THE ESSENTIAL BOOK OF

CHAKRA HEALING

THE ESSENTIAL BOOK OF

CHAKRA HEALING

—

Balance your
vital energies

SAHAR HUNEIDI PALMER

SIRIUS

To Munira Nusseibeh,
who lit my healing pathway;
with love and gratitude.

All images courtesy of Shutterstock,
Unsplash and Adobe Stock.

SIRIUS

This edition published in 2023 by Sirius Publishing, a division of
Arcturus Publishing Limited,
26/27 Bickels Yard, 151–153 Bermondsey Street,
London SE1 3HA

ISBN: 978-1-3988-3010-3
AD010568UK

Printed in China

Contents

Introduction

Chakra healing, self-development and spiritual awakening go hand-in-hand. Our seven major energy centres, or chakras, play a critical role in our overall well-being and can impact not only our physical health, but also our emotional and spiritual states. By balancing and aligning our chakras, we can unlock a deeper understanding of ourselves, increase our self-awareness, and promote positive personal growth.

This ancient practice has knowledge of the human body and energy, and offers a holistic approach to self-development which leads to healing. It can also complement other forms of therapy and treatment. However, the aim of this book is not to diagnose ailments, but to help you understand the inner workings of your body and its connection to your mind and soul. This 'collaboration' is what creates your current condition or emotional state. You will learn how the process of wellness and "dis-ease" (literally not being at ease) work and affect each other and are connected to bigger picture through your breath.

Whether through meditation, visualization, or the use of crystals and aromatherapy, understanding the psychological interpretations of the chakra system is a powerful tool for unlocking our full potential and paving the way for a more fulfilling life. So, take the time to explore your energy centres and embrace the journey towards self-discovery and growth. Chakra healing is not just about physical or emotional wellness, but it's also about spiritual growth and self-discovery. By becoming aware of our energy centres and their associated qualities, we can gain insights into our own patterns of thought and behaviour, and work to realign them with our highest aspirations. By taking charge of our own healing and becoming accountable for our well-being, we can begin to live a life that is true to our purpose and brings us joy and fulfilment.

Moreover, the power of the mind is critical to this process, as our thoughts and beliefs can either support or hinder our growth. We can train our minds to focus on positivity and cultivate the right mindset to support our transformation. When we use our minds to direct our consciousness towards self-improvement, we create a ripple effect that touches all aspects of our lives.

I hope that healing your chakras and engaging in self-development empowers you to create the life you want. By taking an active role in your own healing, you can achieve true, joyful transformation.

Finally, do remember that no book is a replacement for professional medical assistance, so seek it if you need it.

CHAPTER 1
Energy and Matter

"Energy and matter are two sides of the same coin... Match the frequency of the reality you want and you cannot help but get that reality. It can be no other way."

ALBERT EINSTEIN

All matter, living and inanimate, has an energy field. All energy fields communicate together constantly. Furthermore, all energy fields, whether of a person or an animal, a plant or an object, contain information or data within it. When two energy fields (for example, you and another person) interact, information is exchanged; a two-way communication flows between you.

All energy fields are interconnected and communicate with each other.

In energy healing, the energy field of a person is commonly known as the aura (or bio-field). The tangible or manifest element of matter is your physical body, and this is reinforced by its corresponding energy field—your aura. Your aura reflects whatever is happening in your body. And experiences you go through while you are a consciousness in a body is communicated to your aura.

Like Yin and Yang (a metaphor representing the two fundamental principles of all creation), energy and matter are interrelated. If you like, Yin is the unseen energy or essence, or content, and Yang is the manifest state of that energy, form, or container (see Figure 1, overleaf).

When the two aspects come together, or unite, their union forms a third state—the expression of the energy as matter. As a person, the union between consciousness and body makes up your unique personality. In other words, matter is a manifestation of energy.

An example of this in daily life is your ideas. Thoughts are energy which, in conjunction with the appropriate action, take shape and manifest. Your ideas are then made real—or are "realized". Moreover, the reason for the union of two complementing aspects is to enable them to collaborate or co-create. Union enables two separate aspects to experience life as one

Figure 1: Yin and Yang are interrelated.

unit. Separately, they cannot manifest or create—in the same way that your ideas will remain intangible ideas unless you take some action to make them real.

Additionally, a harmonious, balanced union collaborates easily as a whole unit to create or manifest an outcome. In a sense, this collaboration creates a new outcome, which allows for evolution and progress of life. The interaction between them is a continuous cause-and-effect dynamic where whatever affects one, will impact the other.

This book is about the "wholistic" healing of your aura to sustain balance and harmony. The aura has energy centres known as chakras, which are interconnected. For healing to be effective, all aspects of the personality and its environment need to be considered; it is not enough to heal a single chakra. Wholistic healing therefore restores the balance between your body and your energy or consciousness, and enables your life journey to flow with ease to ultimately fulfil your life's purpose.

A state of wholeness creates resonance. A person may feel that they are in a state of bliss, for example. Simply put, as the density of energy, increases, it "solidifies" to become matter. Resonance becomes the force, or bond, that keeps the two aspects together as a whole unit, maintains their optimal function and well-being, and allows them to co-create and evolve. You can apply the same principles to make any personal relationship fulfilling!

Wellness and Dis-ease

Given the interconnected nature of all energy, it follows that as you go about your life, both your body and your energy will be impacted. Healing, or rebalancing and clearing chakras, will be needed every now and then to clear any disturbances that occur as a result of this interaction. You will find methods later on that will enable you to do this. For example, you can make sounds for each chakra that encourage your body and aura to maintain their ideal structure and function. Additionally, chanting such sounds will help your consciousness to easily articulate, or manifest, your ideas, talents, abilities and true voice. Your life becomes an interactive, dynamic and joyful experience as it flows easily, avoiding major obstacles. In other words, your true potential is easily fulfilled.

Furthermore, the personality, which is the union of consciousness and body, engages as a unit with other energy fields such as other people, animals, nature and space. Neither energy nor matter are static. Consequently, your personality is always changing and evolving—as is your energy field. When your physical body expires, however, whatever you

learned while alive remains in your consciousness, adding to the wisdom of collective consciousness. This is because, by definition, energy is indestructible; it transforms from one type of energy to another.

When the harmony of this union is interrupted, both matter and energy are impacted. Matter and energy are hampered because communication between them is obstructed. This state is described as a state of 'dis-ease'.

As a personality, you might experience blockages, restlessness, moodiness and sometimes aches and pains. If the harmony is interrupted for a long time, diseases will occur. Author Caroline Myss famously explained the principle as: "your biography becomes your biology." This is because all that you experience and express is part of who you are and will impact the balance between your physical body and your energy. You will learn more about healing yourself, and what needs to be rebalanced, as you read about the human energy field and the interpretation of each chakra in the following chapters.

There are wider representations of the harmony that can be achieved by healing or taking the right action for either or both aspects of the union between the two collaborating aspects. Figure 2 describes possible interpretations of the two primal forces that unite to be become a "whole," harmonious unit. For example, you and your home, where you are the "content" and your physical space is the "container".

CONTENT	CONTAINER
Energy	Matter
Intangible	Tangible
Essence	Form
Yin	Yang
Soul/consciousness	Physical body
Feminine	Masculine
Mother	Father
Feel of a place	Look and structure
People	Their living space
Goal	Result
Thought/thinking/intuition	Action/doing/logic

Figure 2: The relationship between the aspects of energy and matter.

The Human Energy Field

T he aura of a person is referred to as the Human Energy Field (HEF). In this instance, the physical form, or the body of a person, is the container that holds their corresponding content energy. It represents the expression of their consciousness or soul. Your body and your HEF are two sides of the same coin. It follows that each aspect's energy signature must be compatible with the other. Practically speaking, if you want to manifest a lot of money, for instance, you need to feel, think and behave in terms of that goal in a way that is relevant and consistent.

Moreover, the HEF acts like an energetic, soft memory bank that holds all the information about your biology and biography. It contains the programming about how you have been conditioned to manage different aspects of your life. Imagine that your body is a computer: the hardware is your physical self and the operating system is your thoughts and consciousness. The HEF plugs into the hardware and is accessed by the operating system. Consider energy healing as a way for you to "debug" or clean up distortions within the HEF, thus influencing how the body (computer) functions.

The HEF reflects four main aspects:

✳ **Your body's physical energy and well-being** is
influenced by your diet, level of fitness, ability to
replenish your energy during the day, and the amount
of sleep you get each night for your body to repair itself.
Meditate, take a little nap, or schedule regular time for
enjoyable pursuits and hobbies as a way to recharge
your energy.

✳ **Your emotional energy** goes far beyond your level of
happiness. It represents how you react emotionally to life's
events and how well you process or integrate your life's
experiences so that, for instance, unfavourable situations
don't traumatize you. Additionally, it covers the earliest
emotional programming you have developed since birth
and, in fact, even when you were in the womb.

✳ **Your mental energy** reflects your mental state, thought
processes, understanding and, to some extent, the belief
systems you have formed as a result of your emotional
upbringing and life experiences. For example, if you
worry a lot and experience anxiety, rather than being

able to reason rationally and make wise decisions while dealing with life, this may be the reason.

✳ **Your spiritual energy** includes your motivation for living, your awareness of how you express yourself, and your life's purpose. Your life experiences all come together here, reflecting your self-development and the awareness of your consciousness.

Healing works by restoring harmony between your physical body and your HEF. In other words, by paying attention to the small details as they happen in your daily life, and the decisions you make moment to moment, you can begin to maintain a harmonious life, manifest with ease, and remain on your life path. However, for healing to be effective or complete, you must also do your part. That means, for example, rebalancing yourself regularly, modifying your eating habits or the way you react emotionally to your life experiences, and working on changing beliefs that no longer work for you.

Moreover, becoming consistently aware of your behavioural patterns, and holding yourself accountable to what you are creating in your life, is essential for creating your desired level of well-being. Sometimes this means healing your space, your home, your emotions, modifying your behaviour, or even sorting out your finances (see Chapter 7).

The four main aspects of being human—body, emotions, mind and actions—interact continuously and influence your HEF at every moment. Therefore, the more self-aware you are, and the more you reflect on your experiences, the more you will be in command of your energy system and able to sustain your well-being. Refer to the Seven Chakra System (see Chapter 5), where the interpretation of each chakra will suggest healing remedies to balance it.

How Distorted Patterns are Formed

The combination of your consciousness with your physical body is unique. Your body, brain and consciousness are unique to you. The interaction between them dictates your personality development, to allow your unique personality to emerge as you grow from a newborn to an adult. You have your own unique fingerprints, as well as your own unique voice or sound signature. Your personality has infinite creative abilities because the energy that combines with your body is infinite and connects to other energy fields in the universe. Your potential is infinite, and what you can manifest through this interaction is also infinite. Your mental aspect is what directs the soul-body combination.

As a newborn, you are a body that feels, with no mindset or belief system yet, and for this reason you lack intellectual abilities. Naturally, there will be experiences that you are not capable of dealing with or of knowing how to process. Your responses are emotional and instinctive. Repeated responses to similar experiences leave an imprint in your HEF over time.

Positive imprints enhance your growth into adulthood, while negative ones create distortions or blocks in your HEF. Distorted patterns impede communication between body and the HEF— and as a result your struggle, as a human being, begins.

Initially, the physical body is the first to be affected by what happens in your environment, and by your basic urges such as hunger or thirst, as well as the need to feel safe, secure, and cared for. Your body detects the stimulus from your environment and converts it into electrical signals via the nervous system, and to your brain. Your brain then sends orders back to your glands and organs, activating the relevant hormones, which you express as an emotional reaction. You might start crying if you are hungry. When your needs are not met promptly, you learn to cry for longer. When this pattern is repeated because you do not receive the necessary attention and must always cry for some time, your mind begins to build a belief: "I need to cry for a long time to receive the desired attention and have my needs met."

Over time, you form several beliefs around that initial experience, and this established belief system begins to dictate your actions as you grow up: "I can achieve what I want only if I create a drama to draw attention." This reaction becomes automatic, and if the pattern remains unnoticed, you may maintain this emotional dynamic as you mature due to areas of frozen or stuck energy patterns. When you grow up in a large family with other siblings, for example, you may not receive the same attention as a single child. You may feel unheard or unseen as you try to fit into that life. This triggers an emotional response that leads to the developing of a belief system around false ideas such as "I don't matter", making you feel insignificant or insecure. As a child, you do not yet have a mature cognitive understanding of your circumstances. As a result, if you do not address or consider this pattern as an adult, you will continue to believe and act on that incorrect assumption, feeling insecure or unconfident.

Additionally, parents who constantly argue in front of their children contribute to the development of fearful emotional patterns in their children. The latter develop into a distorted belief system, which might include "relationships are not safe", "I must not express my opinion" or "I must not express how I feel". The disruption of the HEF by such stifling experiences limits a child's personal development and will influence how they perceive the world as they grow. As a result, in order to cope, the child will mask their true feelings and responses, and develop a false identity.

This imbalance not only impedes the child's personal growth and blocks the development of their unique personality,

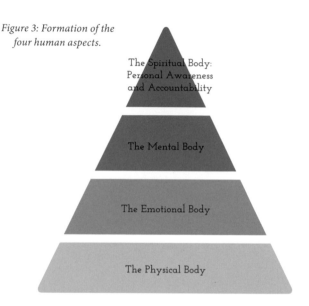

Figure 3: Formation of the four human aspects.

The Spiritual Body: Personal Awareness and Accountability

The Mental Body

The Emotional Body

The Physical Body

but it also literally creates obstacles along their life's journey. Children who learn early to withhold their feelings, grow up unconsciously holding this pattern. This may manifest as speaking softly as an adult if emotional blocks continue to exist undetected. As a grown-up, for example, the person might experience difficulty speaking up in the workplace.

To summarize, all patterns, conducive and destructive, are established in childhood, and remain with you as you grow older, if not identified and modified:

✳ Your body send out and receives signals.

✳ You respond emotionally.

✳ Repeated responses form beliefs.

✳ Consequently, formed beliefs dictate your actions.

The opposite is also true: modifying an action will change a belief, which will modify your emotional reaction. In this situation you begin to feel better or have less difficulty coping with life. Positive patterns reinforce your capacity to develop in a productive way and imply that your distinctive personality will manifest easily, if not spontaneously. Authentic Self is another term that describes your unique identity, or the Real You. Being in alignment describes effortlessly co-creating and evolving, which happens due to ongoing self-awareness and chakra healing.

However, when established patterns are negative, they restrict your view of the world and keep getting in the way of your progress in life. Until you pay attention to them, such distorted energetic patterns will continue to attract recurrent experiences in adulthood because they simply want to harmonize, adjust and balance once more. This is because the natural state is harmony and flow.

Depending on your level of consciousness and stage of life, you will experience these recurring patterns differently. For instance, if as a child you unwittingly developed the pattern that says: "I am unwanted" or "I do not deserve love", you may subsequently feel unlucky in love or in your career later in your life. You might experience the same feelings of rejection with friends at school, at work with colleagues or even in relationships—no matter how much you are actually loved! Until you become aware of it and heal it, the primary theme, or main image, ingrained in your subconscious mind remains: "I do not deserve…" You can combat this by changing your beliefs, which we will look at in more depth in chapter 3.

Frozen Energy

We have learned that our bodies communicate with the HEF, transmitting thoughts and feelings, just as the HEF transmits information from the outside world to our personalities. If you are able to sense auras or perceive them, such distorted patterns appear as dark spots of colour, coarse sensation or cold blocks of frozen energy. Disharmonious vibrations, which have not been integrated in your bio-field, act as impediments to the natural flow of energy and therefore interrupt the synergy between your body–mind system and the outside world.

False beliefs and constrained viewpoints about life that are developed in infancy and childhood are the cause of a history of unhappy relationships, a lack of achievement or ill health. Rather than forming a new belief, such as "I am not what happened to me, I can choose who I want to be", the vibration emanating from the aura continues to be "life is unfair", "I am unfortunate", or "nothing can improve my life". Such vibrations become common scenarios that your subconscious mind dictates and which you play out until you become self-aware and take charge of your own well-being.

Furthermore, repeated experiences help cement beliefs, and beliefs attract experiences. When false (or negative) beliefs go unnoticed, the rabbit-hole becomes even deeper. And the longer these blocks remain, the more likely they are to cause physical dis-ease. In other words, illness starts developing as the energy stops flowing, gains density and changes the physical biology of body cells. Initially, a person begins to experience a lack of vitality due to a sluggish chakra, or random shooting pains, as the block impedes flow and causes physical pain.

Depending on which aspect of your energy field is out of harmony, other signs of blocked or slow energy flow include a confused mind, despair, or a harsh or unforgiving heart.

Aches and pains that come up at random times can be healed quite quickly. Your life force begins to flow when your hands are rubbed together. If you then place your palms on the sore location for a few moments, heat starts to flow towards the sore spot and untangles the distorted energy patterns. There is often immediate relief.

Another technique is to comb through the aura above that location, as if you are running your fingers through it, for a few minutes. Keep doing this until you feel relief. This latter action has also been reported as working well on itchy insect bites.

Personal Awareness and Chakra Healing

To summarize, the physical body senses information from the outside world, and communicates instinctive information to the outside world, such as hunger and thirst. An emotional response is triggered. Repeated emotional response patterns enforce a belief system that consequently dictates actions. Essentially, this interaction is what expresses the personality at each moment.

When you become aware of this dynamic and start taking responsibility to address any required changes, this will transmute negative patterns in your life, and the healing of your chakras begins. Otherwise, such patterns will continue to wreak havoc on your life, enforce negative beliefs further, and influence your mindset to be that of a victim. Your aura vibrates: "I am not responsible for what has happened to me", and your life remains a continuous struggle (see Figure 4).

Figure 4 describes how a balanced aura can be achieved through awareness of the main four human aspects: your physical body, your emotions, your beliefs and your actions.

Such awareness enables energy to flow easily. Without any significant downtime, interacting with life becomes a joyful experience. When distortions, however, go unnoticed, life seems out of control and can impact any aspect adversely.

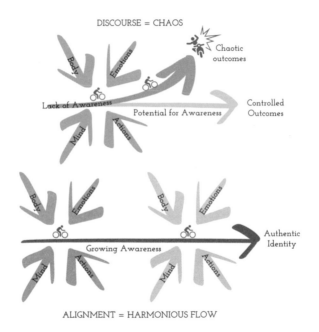

Figure 4: How personal awareness maintains ease of flow.

Your Healing Intention

Truly, healing begins from the moment you become conscious of your subconscious patterns. You can start by healing any current distorted pattern in your life as soon as you become aware of it. Notice which areas trouble you most. Begin now by recording your answers to the following questions:

1   What is the one thing in your life that you would like to change right now? ....
....
....

2   Which human aspect does it fall under: body, emotions, mind or actions? ....
....
....

3   What outcome do you envision when this aspect is healed? ....
....
....

4 What impact on your life would achieving this goal have?...

....

....

....

Finally, why do we need to heal?

We live in a multidimensional universe with many different levels of energy and existence. Every one of us has the ability to have a small impact on the world, for better or worse. Everything we do and believe affects the people in our lives, and their reactions affect others. A seemingly insignificant word gains significance as it passes from person to person, and it can become a source of immense joy, inspiration, fear or suffering.

Your actions and ideas are like throwing stones into still water, causing ripples to spread and expand as they move outward. Your impact on the world is greater than you realize, and the choices you make can have far-reaching consequences. You can direct the ripple effect to make a difference, and send waves of goodwill around the world. The change within each of us as we heal and align with our life path has an impact on everyone around us: the self is the foundation of the many.

CHAPTER 2
The Power
of Breath

"The inner being of a human being is a jungle.
Sometimes wolves dominate,
sometimes wild hogs.
Be wary when you breathe!"

RUMI
Persian poet and Sufi mystic (1207–1273)

Energy flows between the chakras, and between the corresponding auric layers of each chakra. What guides energy flow is your breath. Breathing energises and activates each chakra and helps it to metabolize life's energy into the body and to flow through it. By the same token, shallow breathing dampens a chakra's vibration and limits its function. Just think about it for a moment: you are alive as long as you can breathe! As we age, we move less and stop taking deep breaths. Consequently, we feel less energized or motivated to move, dance or exercise. Effectively, we age faster.

Before oxygen was identified as an element, breathing air was thought to be what powers blood circulation through the heart, and raises a person's vitality, or "spirit", or "animal spirit". Such words were used by the ancient Greeks who explored the human anatomy.

In fact, several ancient cultures knew the HEF and developed their

All that is

BREATH

All that 'I Am'
The Self

Figure 5: Your breath is the link between you and the universe.

own understanding of the human aura and chakra system. In ancient China, for example, it was understood that the physical body has nodes that metabolize energy into the physical body. These form energy pathways, known as meridian lines, where the nodes are known to be acupuncture points. Meridian lines are within the physical body and thought to connect the physical body to the aura.

Ibn al-Nafis (Ala-al-Din Abu al-Hasan Ali ibn Abi-Hazm Qarshi al-Dimashqi) was a thirteenth-century Arab polymath born in Syria. Building on the works and discoveries of his Greek predecessors, he believed that as we breathe, the air enters the lungs and is then mixed in the heart (filtered and oxygenated) to generate the "vital spirit". He wrote an extensive medical encyclopaedia of over 80 volumes, which formed the basis of Western modern medicine, and he is the first person to describe the pulmonary circulation of the blood.

Dr Nayhan Fancy, author of *Science and Religion in Mamluk Egypt*, describes Ibn al-Nafis's work as "the result of two processes: an intensive theoretical study of medicine, physics, and theology in order to fully understand the nature of the living body and its soul"—the physical body and the consciousness inhabiting it. The ancients explored the connection between breath, the physical body and spirit or consciousness.

Shamanism too, for example, recognizes that each chakra in the HEF can be activated by breathing techniques. Life is viewed as a "wheel of sacred dance" that spins effortlessly when we are in balance, allowing for the spontaneous expression of any facet of our personality, in response to the necessities of any given situation. This perspective also considers the integrity of the whole being as a multidimensional dance with an ever-changing dynamic—meaning that at any moment, and according to present circumstance, a personality aspect within us can emerge to help us cope with a situation. In a breath, our personality can change identities as various aspects of our personality can emerge or be expressed.

This dynamic emerges from the spiritual via our psycho-physiological experience—or from the consciousness within our bodies, with each breath. In this way, we experience different aspects of our personalities, referred to as archetypes.

Furthermore, shamans believe that within our lifetime we have a Window of Identity through which we can display our true nature, or the essence or our consciousness —the authentic self. When the authentic self is unable to be articulated because of energy distortions, which can occur at any time within the HEF, obstacles arise. The authentic self is usurped by a fake, masked, identity (the ego) which the current self, or dancer, adopts as its true identity, thus prolonging the struggle. Conversely, when the HEF is balanced, or in alignment, the true self, or the essence of consciousness, is expressed easily. In other words, your path in life unfolds like a carpet rolling out smoothly, and you take the right and appropriate actions to reach your goals, at each moment fulfilling your potential.

Every culture has mythologies and stories of Sacred Dancers who express the two opposing but complementary forces of consciousness within a physical body. Odin, Zeus, the Sun Father, and the Tarot's Emperor all embody the archetype of the container, Yang force, or Father. Demeter, Mary, Earth Mother, Frigg of Norse mythology, and the Empress and High Priestess of the Tarot are all representations of the Mother, or Yin principle of essence. Your awareness of these interrelated energies is what guides your breath and keeps you in touch with your real expression— your true self.

The poet Rumi expressed this beautifully:

The inner being of a human being
is a jungle. Sometimes wolves dominate,
Sometimes wild hogs. Be wary when you breathe!
At one moment gentle generous qualities,
Like Joseph's, pass from one nature to another.
The next moment vicious qualities move in hidden ways.

Wisdom slips for a while into an ox!
A restless, recalcitrant horse suddenly
Becomes obedient and smooth-gaited.
A bear begins to dance.
A goat kneels!
At every moment a new species rises in the chest—
Now a demon, now an angel, now a wild animal.
There are also those in this amazing jungle
Who can absorb you into their own surrender.
If you have to stalk and steal something,
Steal from them!

Breathing Patterns

B ecause breathing patterns are one of the ways we regulate our emotions, they are important. You might hold your breath out of fear or to restrain your tears or anger. Over time, these patterns become ingrained, depleting your body of vitality. What is more, many children experience traumas for which there are no adequate words. Such incidents may have long-lasting effects that serve as blocks of frozen energy throughout adulthood. During adult healing, words, memories and feelings connected to these experiences can be recalled or aroused.

Rumi's elegant poem (see page 43) explains how the aura deviates from balance. Emotional responses give rise to animal selves within us with each breath. When you are an adult and you allow your emotions to run wild, they can control your ideas and behaviours, leading to incredibly painful interior states (or frozen energy). But that doesn't mean you shouldn't express your emotions. You can use your feelings of fear, excitement, rage and grief to help you get through life.

But rather than letting your emotions control you, pay great attention to them—submit, and then let them out through processing. You could punch a pillow, for instance, or write down your emotions while remaining externally unmoved. You will recover control over your emotions once you stop allowing each emotion to tug you in different directions. Your body will rid itself of all misdirected energy and negative thoughts. It will feel light and free, much like a dancer's. You will be able to take slow, deep breaths. The body begins to move unexpectedly freely and fluidly, when healing occurs.

The Sufis, for instance, engage in *Zikr*, or remembering Allah, to banish unfavourable thoughts and draw nearer to the Divine. Zikr is an Islamic meditation practice in which words or prayers are said aloud repeatedly to help the practitioner remember God. Chanting "Hu" (pronounced *who*), which comes from the Arabic for God "Allahu", is one of the most effective forms of meditation in that tradition.

Bioenergetics

All distortions are formed in infancy. A child breathes in fears and holds it within. A child also lacks the right words to express his feelings. However, as an adult, you can now consciously seek to heal. Any blocks will dissolve, rebalancing your aura. Any traumatic experiences will integrate, find their rightful place (in the past) and no longer control how you react. They are no longer memories living within your consciousness. You will find it easier to find the right words to articulate your feelings, releasing any past memories which your present reactions are built upon.

An example of how distorted breathing patterns can affect the physical body is when the ability to speak is hindered until certain physical tensions, within the throat for instance, are relaxed. A person, for example, may feel a lump in the throat or a knot in the stomach, or they may even stutter, which gives the healer or therapist information about what is going on internally within that person.

Dr Alexander Lowen, who developed bioenergetic analysis, recognized this relationship: memories stored within the body affect it physically. He observed the body of his patients and how they walk, their gait and posture, and noticed which group of muscles are chronically contracted or placid. He helped clients to feel and express their emotions more easily by releasing these contractions or mobilizing the underdeveloped areas.

Essentially, bioenergetics release unpleasant memories held in the body, and releases them by vibrating the muscles. The effect is like strumming on the strings of a guitar and is achieved by repetitive movements, such as kicking a mattress while lying on the bed, or mindfully hitting a pillow, moving the hips. When muscle tissue vibrates, it opens the body's energy pathways and releases blocks. Increasing the movement of the body deepens breathing and increases vitality. Any frozen energy can now thaw, restoring unobstructed energy flow.

Keep breathing! Acknowledge any difficult emotion you are going through, and exhale—it's one of the quickest ways to begin healing.

CHAPTER 3
Mind Over Matter

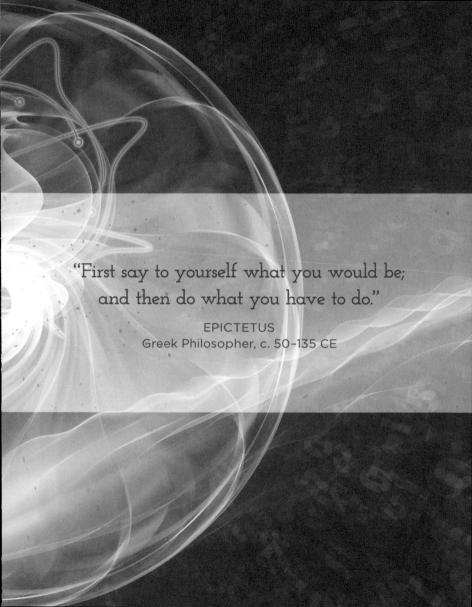

"First say to yourself what you would be;
and then do what you have to do."

EPICTETUS
Greek Philosopher, c. 50–135 CE

S imilar to how a selfie expresses who you are in the moment, taking a metaphorical snapshot of your HEF does the same. Everything in life is vibration, to quote Albert Einstein. Your aura is part of the larger universe, which is constantly changing. Your breathing, feelings and thoughts, as well as how you handle your experiences in life and whether you draw lessons from them, all cause your aura to vibrate continuously.

Vibration implies that anything which seems to be solid is actually moving or vibrating all the time. The tiniest building blocks of our cosmos are vibrating all the time. The appearance of matter as a solid, liquid or gas depends on their velocity (see Figure 5). Energy becomes denser at lower vibrations,

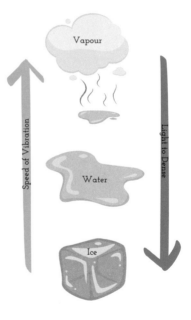

Figure 6: Vibrational speed and density.

eventually solidifying into physical matter. Thoughts are vibrational energy that your mind also transmits. These ideas and thoughts have a vibrational weight. You might get an uplift when you meet a positive individual. On the other hand, you might describe someone as heavy if they are burdened by their thoughts. In a way, even before you can identify it or express it verbally, your aura already conveys your initial impressions.

Whenever you repeatedly use the same words to describe your feelings, your beliefs gain density and eventually manifest as reality. This is how thoughts attract experiences. Emotionally charged words are also enforced by your beliefs and carry weight. As you utter them through your breath, they gain density and materialize. How you feel and think is, therefore, reflected in your auric vibration.

For instance, a person's dense aura, carrying unintegrated frozen energy, may be the reason why they occasionally feel singled out or the target of others' critical behaviour. A person with a dense or low vibration aura because of emotional baggage or a bad attitude, feels "picked" at like you would chip away at an ice block with a pick. Consequently, they will feel mistreated since their energy will reverberate and interact on that level with other people's HEFs. In that sense, negative experiences reflect what is in need of healing. On the other hand, when a person feels uplifted, their aura will resonate with others on a higher frequency.

When you encounter such experiences, ask yourself one of two questions:

* What emotions within me are attracting that behaviour?

* What is this experience showing me?

Instead of asking why this is happening, which implies a victim mindset, rephrasing your enquiry is empowering and may actually reveal the answers you seek. Whatever insights you receive, do not take it personally—it is just energy interacting with yours! Your objective is to heal and uplift your auric vibration.

To summarize, emotional weight is a dense, low vibration. It behaves like ice, representing unprocessed experiences. Unless you resolve them, your ability to engage with your environment through your HEF remains restricted. Consequently, no matter how often you repeat a mantra or an affirmation, emotional weight causes you to wait longer to achieve your goal.

Colour and Sound

Any emotional weight that has been withheld is also released when you are conscious of your breath and let go of it as you exhale. The energy of your thoughts and feelings, which is contained in your aura, influences everything that manifests in your life.

Your voice is uniquely your own. It communicates your vibration as you talk, expressing who you are right now. It also reflects your level of awareness and the overall tone of your aura, in a manner similar to taking a virtual snapshot of your aura. So, be mindful of how you speak to yourself and other people. Your well-being, as well as what you attract and materialize in your life, are greatly impacted by the words you choose to use to communicate your thoughts and feelings.

Your voice is produced by air vibrating via the vocal cords in your throat. It reflects your auric vibration and has a quantifiable distinctive signature. Similarly, your body's cells and organs will continue to function well and reproduce when they are vibrating at their ideal, healthy frequency. Illness and difficulties arise when our cells deviate from their ideal vibration because of energy blocks, or unprocessed experiences

and trauma. Through singing or chanting, as many ancient cultures have done, sound healing is a tool that can assist in balancing the seven chakras.

SOUND VISUALIZATION

Close your eyes and focus mentally on the chakra centre or location where you sense there is an imbalance or pain (see page 81). Try to gain a sense of its frequency. You may imagine or pretend that there is a metronome moving to that frequency. Afterwards, mentally move your focus and your imaginary metronome to a healthy area. According to the metronome, is the vibration of the troubled area accelerating or decelerating?

Synchronize the vibration of the troubled area to that of the healthy one by imagining that your metronome is now beating at the healthy frequency. When you feel that has been achieved, imagine the metronome disappearing but know that you can use it at any time.

Additionally, imagine a metronome at each chakra and synchronize each one with the healthy frequency, starting with chakra 1 and working your way up to chakra 7.

CHAKRA SELF-ASSESSMENT

Figure 7 lists the vibrational sound of each chakra centre. To unblock and restore balance to your aura, practise chanting the sounds that correspond to each vibration.

Take a deep breath in to begin and, as you exhale, chant the chakra's individual sound.

Take a second deep breath, then chant the vibrational sounds of the following chakras in ascending order, concluding with the sound of chakra 7. As you chant, mentally maintain your attention on the location of each chakra to boost the healing's vibratory power. Holding or staring at an image of the colour corresponding to each chakra can help you feel more connected to them:

Notice whether you are able to breathe deeply into that chakra, or not. Consider which chakras are easier to chant, and record your observations below. These reflect your natural abilities.

My balanced chakras are: ....

....

CHAKRA	COLOUR	VIBRATIONAL SOUND	LOCATION
Chakra 1	**Red**	**O** as in *rope*	base of spine
Chakra 2	**Orange**	**OO** as in *due*	just below the naval
Chakra 3	**Yellow**	**AH** in *father*	just under the rib cage
Chakra 4	**Green**	**AY** as in *play*	heart centre, mid chest
Chakra 5	**Blue**	**EE** as in *see*	throat centre
Chakra 6	**Indigo**	**MMMM NNNN**	over bridge of nose
Chakra 7	**Violet**	**NGNGNG** as in *sing*	just above the head

Figure 7: Chakra healing sounds

You will find out more about the interpretation of each chakra in Chapter 5 (see pages 84-5). Come back to what you have written above, and add to what you have learned about yourself.

If your deep breathing is limited—in other words, you run out of breath as you chant a sound—this indicates an imbalance in that chakra. As you practise these sounds for a period of time, the weaker centres will get stronger as they return to balance. Note the chakras that you need to heal below:

My weaker chakra centres are: ....

....

When you chant, the power of your own voice reverberates throughout your body, cleansing and realigning chakra centres. This is an easy and pleasurable chanting technique for opening, cleansing and strengthening your chakras as well as developing your psychic abilities. Sound vibrates with all the cells in your body, making it a pleasant and simple way to fine-tune your instrument. As you continue to practise, you will notice a big improvement—say in a couple of weeks or so. You can use this exercise anytime you feel out of sorts. However, always start with chakra 1 and finish with chakra 7.

The Five Element Theory

A ncient China also developed an important aspect to energy healing called the Five Element Theory. It is a fundamental principle of Traditional Chinese Medicine (TCM). It is useful when talking about chakra healing to also look at the ideas behind this healing modality. It describes the interactions and relationships between things. Wood, fire, earth, metal and water are thought to be the five fundamental elements of everything in the universe through which interactions occur. This interaction can create, control or restrain.

The creation cycle is known as the *Sheng* cycle, where:

✳ Fire is made from wood. Wood is burned to make fire.

✳ Earth is formed by fire. When fire burns, it produces ash, which forms the earth.

✳ Metal is created by the earth. The earth produces the ore from which we make metal tools.

✳ Water is created by metal. Water condenses on metal.

✻ Wood is created by water. Water is necessary for a tree's ability to grow and provide wood.

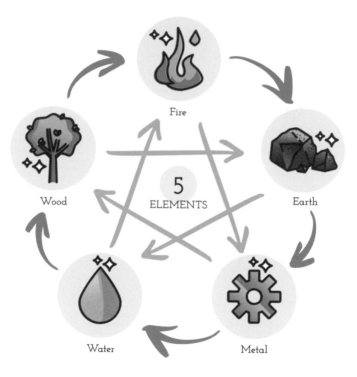

Figure 8: The Five Elements Theory—creation cycle.

The controlling cycle that balances the creation cycle is known as the *Ke* cycle. It describes how each element acts to restrain another in order to maintain balance:

✽ Wood is in charge. Wood is used to shape the earth into a dam.

✽ Earth is in charge. A dam controls the flow of water.

✽ Water regulates. It is used to extinguish fires.

✽ Fire melts metal ore, allowing it to be shaped.

✽ Metal switches wood. To harvest trees for wood, a metal saw is used.

The Five Elements Theory is applied in TCM, philosophy, feng shui, fortune-telling, and martial arts, and for healing and balancing the energy of the physical body's organs. The two cycles represent the two complementing forces, yin and yang, that must remain in balance.

You can also use sound healing with the Five Elements Theory, shown in Figure 9 overleaf.

Wood is associated with the liver and gallbladder. Tendons/ligaments, nails, and eyes are all governed by wood.

The heart, pericardium, small intestine, and triple heater are all associated with **Fire**. Fire is responsible for circulation, complexion and the mind (or Shen).

The stomach and spleen are associated with **Earth**. The earth element is in charge of digestion and muscles.

Metal is linked to the large intestine and the lung. Metal is in charge of the skin/ hair and respiration.

And **Water** is associated with the bladder and the kidneys; and is in charge of elimination, reproduction, and bone formation. Moreover, each element is associated with specific organs and physiological systems.

Figure 9 summarizes the interrelationship between organs and sound according to the TCM and the Five Elements Theory. It highlights the main five organs and their associated vibrational sound. Chanting the sound of each organ balances the chakra centre as well as the area of the body where the organ is restoring balance. You can start with the organ that relates to the current season. Chant each sound as you exhale nine times, or in a multiple of nine.

Take a deep breath in, mentally focus on the location of the organ you are healing, and fully exhale the corresponding organ sound.

ORGAN	ASSOCIATED ORGAN	SOUND	POSITIVE EMOTION	NEGATIVE EMOTION	ELEMENT	SEASON
Lungs	Large intestines	**sssssss**	Courage	Sadness	Metal	Autumn
Kidneys	Bladder	**choooo**	Wisdom	Fear	Water	Winter
Liver	Gall bladder	**shhhhh**	Generosity	Anger	Wood	Spring
Heart	Small intestine	**hawww**	Joy	Impatience/ insincerity	Fire	Summer
Spleen	Stomach/ pancreas	**whooo**	Fairness/ balance	Worry	Earth	Indian summer

Figure 9: The vibrational healing sound of organs in the Five Element Theory.

CHAPTER 4
Sensing Auras

"There are more things in
Heaven and Earth, Horatio,
Than are dreamt of in your philosophy."

SHAKESPEARE'S *HAMLET*, ACT 1 SCENE 5, 165–66

With practice, your ability to see auras will improve. This entails practising patience, letting go of any expectations and softening your gaze. If you cannot immediately see auras, you may frequently feel their quality instinctively. For instance, you feel comfortable around someone who seems to "glow". You can get unsettling feelings, on the other hand, when someone passes by or enters your personal space for no apparent reason.

Additionally, several colours can appear in a single aura at any time. Even so, depending on the underlying main influences at the time, you might notice one dominant colour when looking at a photograph of your aura. The aura reflects your actions and your emotional, mental and physical health. You can do the following exercise to see auras:

✳ Position your subject against a solid, light-coloured background. Alternatively, to observe your own aura, stand at least 60 cm (2 feet) away from a mirror with a soft light source behind you (the bathroom might be a good place).

✳ Rub your hands together to energize your own energy, and regulate your breath as you gaze softly at your subject or your own reflection.

✳ Pay close attention to the area between the shoulder and the neck. Maintain a gentle focus on this area while remaining relaxed and open to perceiving any information without straining your eyes.

✳ You may notice a white or clear light at first around the head, neck and shoulders. But, as you extend your eyeline out to the rest of your body, while you maintain a soft gaze, this glow will begin to appear in colour.

It takes time to see auras, so be patient and practise with a variety of friends. Keep honing your skills. When you are successful, you might observe any of the auric colours, or a combination of them. Colour is a vibration of light, and prominent colours in the aura carry an interpretation:

Red represents someone who is active, adventurous, and courageous. Someone who is well-grounded, energetic and strong-willed. A red that is dark and murky can also describe someone who is quick to anger or to lose their temper.

Orange represents a thoughtful, considerate person, a passionate creative or successful and friendly type. It may indicate that the subject is pregnant. Dark cloudy orange can reflect ignorance and a sluggish flow, with problems around sex organs or achieving the life they want.

Yellow represents an intelligent and logical person, possibly a writer or a teacher. They are skilled observers and critical thinkers, as well as self-sufficient. On the negative side, a murky colour with dark spots can represent an irresponsible, immature or unstable person.

Pink represents a kind, compassionate and loving personality who enjoys the company of others. A person who has a healing presence, is sensitive, sensible and aware. A cloudy pink colour can reflect a weak immune system or immaturity.

Green represents a creative, hardworking and nurturing individual. They are good communicators and can make great leaders. They are well-liked, charitable and health-conscious. Brown-black or greyish green can reflect envy, a blocked heart centre, jealousy or guilt.

Blue represents communication skills and intuitive abilities such as mediumship. It may indicate someone with many ideas and visions. These individuals are also extremely intuitive and intelligent. They have a strong emotional foundation and are natural motivators and inspirers. At times, they may be workaholics and manipulators.

Not everyone who works as a healer can see colour. You can, however, train yourself to sense the vibration and the qualities of chakras, by becoming acquainted with the feel of each colour and each chakra. The vibration of each chakra changes as energy rises from the dense physical first chakra to the spiritual lighter seventh chakra.

The frequency of vibration is what determines the colour of each chakra and its quality when you sense it. With practice, you will be able to detect any blockage which creates distorted patterns. Keep an open mind about what you perceive, as perception abilities vary from person to person.

Perceiving Chakra Colours

Tuning into the seven colours of chakras is a one way of enhancing your sensory perception. The vibration of each colour holds a lot of information. To sense the vibration of colour, practise sensing each of the seven colours in their respective order, by passing your palm over a set of colour cards. Begin your colour sensing adventure by carefully considering each colour before moving on to the next. Allow yourself enough time for each colour and avoid distractions. Make your own deck of colour cards for this purpose, by referring to colours that correspond to each chakra.

Another option is to look for light films, which are commonly used to change the colour of stage lights. Place a colour film on a window or under a light source and take notes as you sense the light emanating from each filter. Also, try to sense each colour card or film just by running your palm over it or holding it between your palms and meditating on it.

Pay attention to any physical sensations you feel, or any visual images or thoughts. Write your observations below as you explore and perceive each colour, along with any ideas that occur to you as you write. When you begin healing, this reference will be crucial to you because it will provide you with a lot information.

Red: ....

....

....

....

Orange: ....

....

....

....

Yellow: ....

....

....

....

Green: ....

....

....

....

Blue: ....

....

....

....

Indigo: ....

....

....

....

Purple: ....

....

....

....

Once you are familiar with what each colour feels like, ask a friend or a partner to be a volunteer. Then try to sense the aura of that person.

Energizing Your Chakras

Chakras spin within us as they process energy as a result of the interplay between our consciousness and our physical body. If you like, our unique personality is the result of this combination between energy and matter. They are centres of activity which help us receive information, process an incoming life force and facilitate our understanding.

Moreover, chakras transmit life energies, as well as our thoughts and emotions. When they are functioning well, they help us materialize our well-being, create new life experiences and achieve our goals. To sustain their function, energy needs to be able to flow easily into and out of each chakra to the next. So, when a chakra is functioning well, interacting with the outside world or the Universal Energy Field (UEF), a joyful life materializes naturally.

Physical activity and mindful breathing, for example, are the simplest of ways of energizing your chakras. Going for a walk in nature—a forest or a green field, for example— allows you to breathe more deeply and reduces your anxiety. Your aura is energized as a result of the interaction between your HEF and other energy fields in nature, making you feel refreshed. During your walk, your aura recycles any frozen energy and rebalances distorted energetic pattern. Gradually, you experience a sense of letting go as balance is restored. Sitting under a tree with your back to the trunk, taking deep breaths of fresh air and mindfully breathing out fully, is a quick and simple way to rebalance.

Chakra healing does not always have to be a time-consuming process. Healing can sometimes take the form of mindfully breathing out such blocks. Simply put, breathing powers the HEF. Drawing your attention to your breathing pattern can be an effective tool to increasing your vitality and releasing distorted energy pathways.

The physical body reflects energy blocks, which are stored as cellular memory, affecting a person's structure, posture or gait. A person with low self-esteem would walk with their back arched inwards, for example, protecting their solar plexus and avoiding direct exposure to the outside world. Droopy shoulders can be an indication of someone with a long history of carrying the weight of the world on their shoulders.

As a healer, when a chakra is slow, or functioning below optimum frequency, you may sense or perceive that as a murky colour, a cold or coarse sensation, or a slow vibration. What it means is that collaborating with the outside world becomes a struggle. Eventually, distorted and unmetabolized energy takes its toll on a person's health. This understanding will help you devise your healing plan.

CHAPTER 5
The Seven Chakra System

"We are all connected; to each other, biologically. To the earth, chemically. To the rest of the universe atomically. We are not figuratively, but literally stardust."

NEIL DEGRASSE TYSON
Astrophysicist, Planetary Scientist, Author

The Auric Field

The chakra system was developed in India between 1500 and 500 BCE in the oldest text known as the Vedas. In modern times, the Seven Chakra System was first described by Purnananda Swami of Bengal, in 1577 in his famous book *Sat-Cakra-Nirupana*, which Sir John Woodroffe translated in English and published in his book *The Serpent Power* in 1919. In 1968, Christopher Hills' book *Nuclear Evolution* was published and he was responsible for linking the chakras to the colour spectrum. Each chakra has its own unique density, frequency, sound and colour.

Your aura is composed of seven primary energy layers, or energy bodies, that radiate externally from your physical body one on top of the other. The word aura is derived from the Greek word for 'wind', reflecting your dynamic moods and feelings, and the ever-changing overall vibe.

Each auric layer is linked to the next by an energy vortex called a chakra. If you were able to see auras, chakras would be like wheels of colour along the front or back of the body. Their name is derived from the Sanskrit word for 'wheel'. Think of chakras as body energy centres through which vital life force

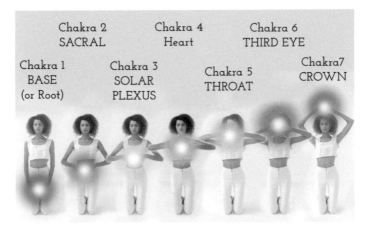

Chakra 2
SACRAL

Chakra 4
Heart

Chakra 6
THIRD EYE

Chakra 1
BASE
(or Root)

Chakra 3
SOLAR
PLEXUS

Chakra 5
THROAT

Chakra7
CROWN

Figure 10: Locations and colours of the seven chakras.

energy is metabolized and then flows from one centre to the next, energizing every cell and organ in your body. There are, however, numerous tiny chakras, or energy vortices, within the physical body. Think of them as the acupuncture points along small energy pathways, that run throughout the physical body known as the meridians.

Every chakra has a unique auric layer, or body. Every auric layer has its own set of seven chakras, each located in the same place on the body. Together the seven auric bodies comprise a complex energy matrix. The etheric body of the first chakra, for instance, is the first layer of energy close to the physical body. The first chakra connects to the next auric layer of the second chakra, the emotional body. And so on, like an octave of auric layers extending outwards away from the body.

Essentially, the HEF (see page 18) mirrors the biology of your physical body. Each of your seven personal chakras spin and radiate outwards. Together the chakras run up the spinal cord from the base to the crown of the head. The specific location of a chakra corresponds to the function of a gland within our physical body, a major nerve plexus and their respective biological activities, such as reproduction, digestion, breathing, immune system, speaking seeing and mental activity, respectively (see Figure 11, pages 84-5). It follows that each chakra corresponds to different psychological and emotional needs as well.

A chakra metabolizes incoming energy to nurture the physical body with vital life force. We are able to navigate our lives because our brain senses signals from the outside world. Information is fed through the chakras to the nervous system along the spine and towards the brain. In turn, our brain sends instructions to various glands and organs to help us cope. Such operations are reflected in our aura. Understanding the chakras' dynamic helps us to understand ourselves on a deeper level.

The Seven Chakra System

The seven chakra system is therefore a metaphor that explains our interpersonal network, and ultimately assists in grasping how we operate as consciousness energy in a physical body. It helps us understand the effect we experience in our lives.

As layers of HEF continue to vibrate outwards through more complex layers of chakra energy fields, we ultimately connect our personal aura to what is referred to as the Universal Energy Field (UEF) that we live in (which extends to the source of all energy). This direct connection between the chakra system, glands and organs offers a psychological interpretation that helps us understand our life dynamic (see Figure 11).

Aura colours have a significance because each colour represents a distinct dimension within our energy field.

The way these colours change and interact represents your **emotional**, **spiritual** and **physical** complexities, as well as events throughout your life. Figure 12 (page 86) demonstrates the locations of the seven chakras and their colours.

CHAKRA	CORRESPONDING GLAND	PSYCHOLOGICAL (HORMONAL) FUNCTION
Chakra 1: Root	**Adrenals**	Survival
Chakra 2: Sacral	**Gonads**	Sex
Chakra 3: Solar Plexus	**Pancreas**	Power
Chakra 4: Heart	**Thymus**	Love
Chakra 5: Throat	**Thyroid**	Communication
Chakra 6: Brow	**Pituitary**	Imagination
Chakra 7: Crown	**Pineal**	Spirituality

Figure 11: Hormonal and psychological functions of chakras.

CORRESPONDING AURIC LAYER BODY	CONNECTS TO	ELEMENT	ESSENCE	COLOR
Etheric	Physical Body and cellular structure	Earth	**I Am Alive**	**Red**
Emotional (Personality Aspect)	Emotional and Physical Body	Water	**I Feel** (mood and lower ego)	**Orange**
Mental (Personality Aspect)	Physical and Mental Body	Fire	**I Achieve**	Yellow
Astral (bridge to spiritual plane)	Emotional and Physical Body	Air	**I Love**	**Green**
Etheric Template (blueprint of the physical body)	Emotional and Mental Body	Sound	**I Express** (ego)	**Blue**
Celestial (Emotional body of spiritual aspect)	Mental, Emotional and Spiritual (Ego-spiritual) Body	Light	**I, The Visionary**	**Indigo**
Ketheric (Mental body of spiritual aspect)	Spiritual Body	Thoughts	**I Am Connected**	**Violet**

Chakras 2 to 6 also operate on the back of the body as indicated in Figure 12 opposite. Chakras on the front of the body help us perceive the world we face and the back chakras help us to express our unique essence into the world.

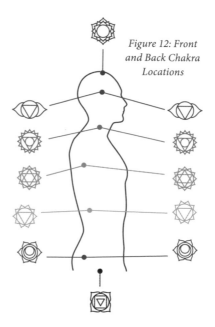

Figure 12: Front and Back Chakra Locations

Note that the root chakra (1), is located just below the spine (between the legs), and the crown chakra (7), is located just above the head. The root chakra is the main connection to the earth.

When we are firmly grounded, vital life force travels up the spine, nurturing each chakra above. Our physical health thrives and we are motivated to grow and live our lives. Chakra 7 receives vital energy into the head, inspiring us with ideas and thoughts.

For example, chakra 1, the root chakra, corresponds to the adrenal glands responsible for fight or flight. Its psychological function is survival; it connects to the etheric body which mirrors the physical body, and the mental auric layer that surrounds the body (the beliefs you hold about life, your health and physical body). So, its essence is 'I am alive', as chakra 1 metabolizes energy from the HEF to maintain our survival.

Essentially, the HEF mirrors the biology of your physical body. Each of your seven personal chakras are located at, and correspond to, the glands within your physical body and their respective biological functions and emotional instinctive responses such as reproduction, digestion, breathing, immune system, speaking, seeing, fight or flight, and mental activity. Additionally, each chakra also corresponds to different psychological needs and emotions, as well as an auric layer of the energy body.

The Auric Layers of the Energy Body

C hakras are directly linked to any pathology in the body since they function to vitalize the physical body. Each chakra metabolizes energy from the UEF, which passes through to the meridians (or *nadis*) and is transmitted to the corresponding gland, which is associated with a physiological function, and to the organ along that meridian. This connection yields the essence of each chakra and provides a structured function for the auric layers (see Figure 13).

On the following pages, we look at the connection of each auric layer radiating outwards from the body to each chakra. Auric bodies of chakras 1 to 3 relate to the physical plane, our personal development as we grow from a newborn to an adult. From the heart chakra 4 onwards, the auric layers relate to the spiritual plane. Chakra 4 is thought of as a bridge between the physical and spiritual planes. Auric layers of chakras 5 to 7 relate to the spiritual plane.

Barbara Brennan, pioneer of Bioenergetic Healing, explains in her book *Hands of Light*, that every chakra in the etheric body

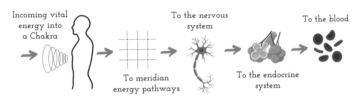

Figure 13: Metabolic Process of Energy into the Physical Body

has a direct connection to the same chakra in the finer body that surrounds and interpenetrates it. The chakras in the emotional body are linked to those in the mental body, the next finer body, and so on for all seven layers. Understanding the body's auric layers can help us better understand how we transition from a personality in a physical body to a spiritual consciousness.

AURIC LAYERS OF THE PHYSICAL PLANE

Think of chakras as seven great force centres where there are seven great nerve ganglia in the physical body, in the astral body, as well as in the body of the consciousness (or soul) which we are going to refer to as the spiritual body. The spiritual body is expressed predominantly through the upper four chakras. The physical body is predominantly expressed through the lower three chakras. However, all seven bodies of energy are located within the physical body radiating outwards.

Think of the bottom three auric layers as being connected to the personality or physical world, and the top three layers as connected to the spiritual world. All energies must pass through the astral layer, which is connected to the heart chakra, in order to move from one realm to another.

The heart is where the incoming energy from the crown chakra, through to the throat chakra, must travel before it can be altered and metabolized by the personality, or the lower three chakras. Similarly, energy from the lower three chakras must pass through the heart, which is the seat of universal or unconditional love for all consciousness, to be transmuted into spiritual energy.

Our consciousness is therefore, expressed through these seven spinning chakras as areas of mind power. When awareness flows through any one or more of these areas, certain functions happen such as the function of memory, the function of reason, the function of willpower and so forth:

The Etheric Body — First Layer

The transitional state between energy and matter is known as ether. It is the closest to the body, has the same structure as the physical body and contains all the organs. The physical matter of the body tissue is shaped and anchored on a specific structure made up of lines of energy. The matrix for cell growth is created by the etheric structure, which is formed prior to the physical body.

The Emotional Body — Second Layer

This layer has coloured clouds of fine substance in continual fluid motion, in contrast to the structured etheric body. It is associated with the emotions of a person. A clairvoyant might see brilliant colours, for instance, if they are associated with positive emotions like love, joy or excitement; otherwise, colours would appear muddy or dark. It also contains emotions of self-acceptance and self-love.

The Mental Body — Third Layer

This layer is a structured lemon-yellow light layer, composed of thoughts, habitual thought forms and mental processes (rational clarity balanced with intuitive mind). It is bright yellow, radiating from the head and shoulder and extending around the whole body. It also contains other colours from the emotional layer which reflect the emotions associated with a thought. Strong thought forms, whether positive or negative ones, do affect how we feel and this in turn will affect our decision making.

AURIC LAYER OF THE ASTRAL PLANE
The Astral Level — Fourth layer

This is the level where we co-create things to realize them into the physical world. It is composed of colourful clouds of emotional plasma and is associated with how we feel about each other, and all beings. The colours of the heart chakra are often referred to as green and pink. Green is the colour on the first physical body. However, the heart chakra of a loving person will be seen to be full of rose light on the astral level. (Green is the frequency of personal love, or love on a physical plane and rose is the frequency of higher love for all consciousness, on a universal level.) Grief over deceased loved ones, for example, can be present in this body. Through this layer, astral travel is possible and we also send and receive positive or negative streams of love from here.

AURIC LAYERS OF THE SPIRITUAL PLANE
The Etheric Template — Fifth Layer

This body encompasses every shape and structure that exists on the physical level as an energy blueprint or template. To a clairvoyant, it's like a photographic negative. At this level, sound makes matter. Sound therapy works well on this layer. This level is structured, just like the fifth chakra.

The Celestial Body — Sixth Layer

The sixth auric layer is fluid. It is a spiritual plane's emotional level. We feel spiritual bliss at this level. This layer has a golden opalescent quality. A person can experience unrestricted love when their heart chakra is open and energy flows freely through it. It stores all memories of past experiences as energetic patterns. This layer is associated with enlightenment, or cosmic consciousness, where the unconscious and conscious become one.

The Ketheric Template (Causal Body) — Seventh Layer

Inspiration and guidance flow through this mental body of the spiritual plane. It contains every auric body linked to the current personality. It is very structured and resembles a golden-silver resilient light grid. It includes the person's present life plan and the past lives they are seeking to clear in this lifetime.

As you may have noted, even-numbered auric bodies and chakras are flexible, while odd-numbered ones are structured. This keeps the body's and the bio field's energy flowing. When it comes to healing, a healer will also assess the flow in the chakras below and above that chakra to rebalance flow that is obstructed or not working at its best.

CHAKRAS AND ANGEL ENERGY

There are various forms or schools of healing that work with chakras. One of these is that of connecting the chakras with angel energies. Dr Gaetano Vivo (gaetanovivo.com) is a Reiki Master and teacher in the Usui/Tibetan and Karuna Reiki systems in addition to his ground-breaking Xantia Healing, which combines vibrational healing, crystal therapy, chakra balancing, and spiritual guides and angels.

He has a created a method of teaching and seeing the chakras and the angels associated with each, where each angel energy helps with a specific emotion as follows (see Figure 14).

CHAKRA	ANGEL ENERGY	EMOTION
1: Root	Sandalfon	Helps to ground and build a stronger connection to the earth.
2: Sacral	Gabriel	Communication, creativity and sexuality.
3: Solar Plexus	Uriel	Anxiety, depression, not feeling good about yourself and experiencing pure joy.
4: Heart	Raphael	Pure Love, for self and others, healing wounded hearts, abandonment, rejections, losing loved ones.
5: Throat	Michael	Helps to cut all the cords related to negative emotions in people.
6: Brow	Metatron	Connection to the window of the soul, the psyche, the unknown, the spiritual world.
7: Crown	Chamuel	Connection to the source of Divine white light.

Figure 14: Angels and Chakras

Chakras 1, 2 and 3
THE FOUNDATION OF PERSONALITY

The psychological interpretation of chakras explains and assists us in grasping how we operate as consciousness, or energy, in a physical body. In other words, they help us to understand the effects of our experiences. The first three chakras represent how the personality emerges, and how life experiences create emotional and mental patterns. Without awareness, gaining wisdom from our life's experiences would not be possible and we would not be able to direct our consciousness as we grow up and lay the foundations of our personality. This means that any current emotional weight in our aura which has not been integrated or healed will impede our personal growth and create blocks or 'dis-ease'.

Figure 15 describes the seven chakras' psychological rights. When a chakra is functioning well and balanced, its psychological right is expressed fully, reflecting its essence.

ROOT CHAKRA 1 — THE RIGHT TO HAVE
The etheric body or layer is connected to this chakra, which

CHAKRA	PSYCHOLOGICAL INTERPRETATION	PSYCHOLOGICAL RIGHT
1: Root	Survival	The right to have
2: Sacral	Sex	The right to feel
3: Solar Plexus	Power	The right to act
4: Heart	Love	The right to love and be loved
5: Throat	Communication	The right to speak and hear the truth
6: Brow	Imagination	The right to see
7: Crown	Spirituality	The right to know

Figure 15: Psychological Rights of Chakras

has a red vibration. It serves as the energetic framework for the formation of each person's unique personality. It is situated at the base of the spine and connected to the kidneys, genital organs and adrenal glands. Internal organ, bone, muscle, blood, and bladder development are all influenced by it. Chakra 1 represents the element of Earth, because it grounds our consciousness in our physical body. A lack of vitality and general weakness, especially in the legs, could be symptoms of low energy in this chakra, along with rheumatism, arthritis and other related conditions.

Chakra 1 symbolizes the psychologically fundamental underlying beliefs about family, security and collective safety. If we are denied the basic essentials of survival, such as food, clothing, a healthy atmosphere and physical touch, we will doubt that right throughout our lives in connection to many things, including money, possessions, love, and time to ourself.

Unblocking Chakra 1:

The following elements are related to chakra 1: having a healthy body and looking after with a healthy diet and regular activity; your home enviroment and feeling secure; your business, including having a clean and organized desk, filing system and new business cards; improving your network and connections, taking care of finances; your possesions, decluttering, giving away what you do not need; loving and enjoying what you have or buy; the Earth, walking in nature, and taking care of the environment.

Affirmation of Chakra 1:

I feel firmly rooted, safe and secure in my life.

SACRAL CHAKRA 2 — THE RIGHT TO FEEL

Located in the pubic area in the front, and the kidneys at the back, this chakra vibrates orange. It is associated with the primary sexual organs and both the physical process of conception and the powerful psychological urges which are the hallmark of sexual maturity in humans. It also relates to the small and large intestines, and thus how well we digest or assimilate life. It is also related to menopause, teenage development, period pains and infertility.

The second chakra represents emotions and relates to the water element, as emotions are as fluid as water. Thus, blame, guilt, money, sex, power, creativity, ethics and honour are also associated with chakra 2. This chakra's quality reflects life's vital force within a person — the ability to sense life experience, react and express emotions. It also reflects or represents the child within. What blocks chakra 2 is a culture where emotional expressiveness is frowned upon.

Unblocking Chakra 2:

The second chakra is where the upward-moving energy current splits into two to express our uniqueness through making choices and creating. Chakra 2's primary theme is transformation and change that opens up new opportunities. For instance, accepting change can help us advance, much as swimming in water enables the body to be flexible and feel free, letting joy in and letting go of shame and guilt. Additionally, since consciousness is creative, it's imperative to have a fulfilling creative interest that you can accomplish independently. Chakra 2 healing includes cultivating real relationships and connections with others where you say what you mean and mean what you say.

Affirmation of Chakra 2:
I connect to others naturally. I have the power to create and transform easily.

SOLAR PLEXUS CHAKRA 3 — THE RIGHT TO ACT

After splitting in Chakra 2, the upwards-moving energy current rejoins to create the power of Yin and Yang in chakra 3. The individual is empowered to assert their unique personality, talents and gifts. Chakra 3 vibrates with a yellow colour and is located near the solar plexus in the front of the body, and behind the adrenals at the back. When this centre is clogged or weak, the digestive organs suffer.

A person may also have doubt, fears, anxiety and low self-esteem or find it difficult to make decisions, or to manifest their goals in the physical world due to being overshadowed or influenced by other people's views (rather than believing in their own power or uniqueness). Chronic fatigue, inability to breathe deeply, weakened immune system, coffee and sugar addiction, cravings for alcohol, tranquillizers and opiates are all symptoms of a depleted third chakra.

Chakra 3 is associated with the element of fire, which represents the fiery energy of creating, planning and acting to manifest our goals. A well-developed third chakra helps a person feel empowered to face responsibilities to all those who need help — people and animals. This feeling of empowerment comes without control or the abuse of power, meaning that a person hones their emotional outbursts and is able to assert themselves calmly.

Unblocking Chakra 3:

Chakra 2's emotional work involves acknowledging and releasing emotions of victimization, while chakra 3 is about claiming the responsibility that our lives are the result of our own free will. Unblocking this chakra involves standing your ground, protecting what is sacred within, not abusing power, accepting life's challenges, being assertive in a quiet way without conflict, and being willing to fight, if need be, but avoiding it as much as possible. Additionally, laughter and finding your sense of humour is a great for releasing anger and allowing the empowerment current to rise through the third chakra.

Affirmation of Chakra 3:

I am free to be me, and I am the power and the authority in my life.

Chakra 4
THE ADULT NOW

We enter the domain of spirit that permeates all matter as we move into the upper chakras' more etheric levels. The transcendence of the lower chakras (training the ego and allowing the true self to emerge) and the immanence of the upper spiritual chakras are integrated into one experience when a higher level of awareness and understanding is reached. The personality becomes the true expression of the consciousness. Transcendence teaches us to reach beyond our boundaries and to get some distance that might help us view things from a different perspective.

HEART CHAKRA 4 — THE RIGHT TO LOVE AND BE LOVED

The Heart chakra symbolizes the psychological growth of the personality from chakra 1 to chakra 3. At this level of awareness, it represents how the personality operates and expresses itself in the present, on its way to connecting with higher (spiritual) consciousness more deeply. When open, the person operates from the heart — authentically and lovingly.

The element of chakra 4 is air, representing ease of connection to all consciousness and planes of consciousness.

Moreover, energetically, the heart is the cauldron that transmutes all obstacles and imbalances, and balances personality with spirit. Here forgiveness, respect and acceptance, of self and other consciousness, are the keys to transcending the duality of the physical plane. It also serves as a hub for establishing connections to the universe and engaging in astral travel.

The heart centre balances our bodily and spiritual aspects, vibrates in green and is positioned at the heart, front and back. The personality and spiritual aspects are balanced and unified by the heart centre. When thought is formed by the personality, it is released into the astral plane. The astral plane is also the realm of where the imagination, dreams and creative thought begin to take form. It expresses the capacity to love everyone and everything unconditionally — beyond the self. Here the ego of the personality starts to dissolve, and the higher, wiser spiritual aspect is activated as we become more aware. When chakra 4 is operating at its optimum, energy flows easily in and out of it, and the personality authentically expresses its essence.

Unblocking Chakra 4:

Unblocking this chakra requires both forgiving the self and others, unconditionally loving your inner child and practising self-love, which includes not being self-critical! In addition, chakra 4 can be healed through deep breathing and letting go of previous thought patterns and emotions that led to unpleasant experiences.

Affirmation of Chakra 4:

I easily give and receive love. I completely release old patterns that created heartache in my life.

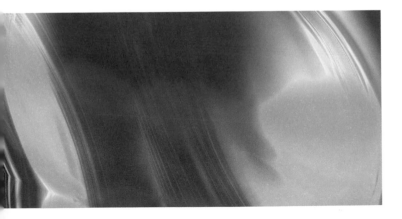

Chakras 5, 6 and 7
THE SPIRITUAL SELF

On this level, energy shapes that are in resonance with one another frequently stay harmonious, as though bound by the force of entrainment. Telepathic communication, vibrational healing and the ability of music to evoke highly altered states of consciousness are examples of this principle in action.

THROAT CHAKRA 5 — THE RIGHT TO SPEAK AND HEAR THE TRUTH

The fifth chakra, which is situated in the front and rear of the throat, is linked to psychic communication and inner guidance, as well as inner hearing, speaking, smelling and tasting. It stands for the capacity to recognize and accept true insights as well as the ability to perceive and trust our inner guidance. By fine-tuning our own vibrational energies, we may express ourselves more clearly and communicate with others more effectively. Chakra 5 is associated with the element of sound, listening to our intuition and recognizing that all creativity is a form of communication. Through communication we create our lives and circumstances, and live in general harmony with our surroundings.

Unblocking Chakra 5:

Conscious self-control and discipline, living in harmony with the One's truth, and understanding that every thought has the potential to be a tool for good or a tool to cause injury. Realizing that positive thoughts result in the communication of ideas and manifestation of intentions are all key actions to unblocking the fifth chakra.

Affirmation of Chakra 5:

My voice is heard and I openly express myself, my creativity and ideas with truth and clarity.

BROW CHAKRA 6 — THE RIGHT TO SEE (THE TRUTH)

The sixth chakra, sometimes referred to as the third eye, is our inner guidance system and is situated in front and behind the pituitary gland. It is associated with the element of light (enlightenment) and oversees the other main chakras in that respect. When closed, we are unaware of our own truth, unable to express our skills or abilities effectively, unable to gather insight from life's experiences, and unable to envision or dream of a better future. Understanding and recognizing patterns is a necessary component of learning to see. It represents mental clarity, memory, imagination, the capacity to recall dreams, and the capacity to think symbolically and see patterns. It acts on the higher mental plane — the ability to conceptualize, visualize and project.

Unblocking Chakra 6:
Understanding our dreams, applying sound judgement, accepting our inner knowing, creating visual art, claiming our capacity for imagination, and having a clear mental and intellectual vision of our lives are all aspects of working with the sixth chakra.

Affirmation of Chakra 6:
I have a clear view of everything, I am open to my inner wisdom. I can make my vision into reality.

CROWN CHAKRA 7 — THE RIGHT TO KNOW (THE TRUTH)
Chakra 7 is the top major chakra, often known as the crown. It is placed right above the crown of the skull and is linked to spiritual connection, growth, channelling and receiving inspiration. It is related to the element of thought — the ability to integrate our life.

Unblocking Chakra 7:

Hold your arms above your head. Imagine fluffing your hair by combing through it with your fingers. Visualize violet light illuminating your crown chakra. Imagine it as being on the verge of the visible spectrum, bridging the visible and invisible realms. In addition, close your eyes and mentally focus over your head. Breathe deeply into the seventh chakra and release any blockages as you exhale. Use the chakra sound *Lao* for the crown chakra.

Affirmations of Chakra 7:

I am always connected to the highest source of guidance. My inner wisdom guides me to my highest good. Life is my teacher.

Think of chakras as seven great force centres where there are seven great nerve ganglia in the physical body, in the astral body, as well as in the body of the consciousness (or soul) which we are going to refer to as the spiritual body. The spiritual body is expressed predominantly through the upper four centres or chakras.

The astral body is predominantly expressed through the lower three centres or chakras. However, all seven bodies of energy are located within the physical body radiating outwards. Our consciousness is, therefore, expressed through these seven spinning chakras, which are actually areas of mind power. When awareness flows through any one or more of these areas, certain functions happen, such as the function of memory, the function of reason and the function of willpower.

Your auric bodies serve as a sort of memory bank, storing your programming for how you handle various aspects of your life. It connects to the physical body's hardware through the chakras. Your awareness and thoughts are the operating system of the drive. Self-awareness is the essential healing work to address the system's issues and debug it. When healing, bear in mind that a deficient chakra will also affect the performance of the chakra above it and below it. Keep a 'wholistic' healing approach whenever you are rebalancing.

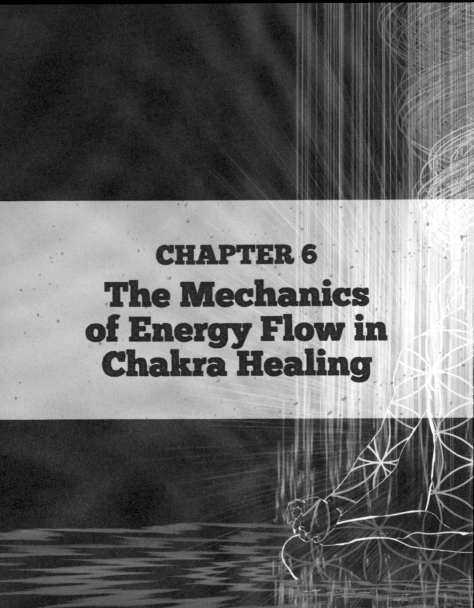

CHAPTER 6
The Mechanics of Energy Flow in Chakra Healing

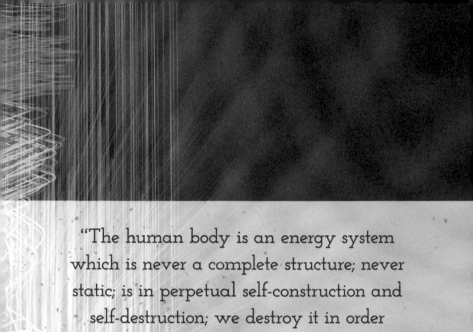

"The human body is an energy system which is never a complete structure; never static; is in perpetual self-construction and self-destruction; we destroy it in order to make it new."

NORMAN OLIVER BROWN (1913–2002)
Scholar, Writer, and Social Philosopher

You can locate any potential imbalances or obstructions within the aura by using the seven chakra system as a template for healing and rebalancing. To start the healing process, we must become empowered to make the necessary changes through self-awareness. More importantly, the ultimate objective is to maintain your equilibrium and actualize your life's purpose. Healing begins as soon as you start paying attention to your emotional responses, especially during an emotionally charged circumstance.

For example, do you have trouble expressing yourself? Do you typically hold your breath and speak softly? Or do you express your thoughts and feelings easily? Additionally, pay attention to how you walk and your posture. Notice whether your body moves freely, and if your feet are planted firmly on the ground, or do you tread lightly on your toes? The latter is an indication of how well the first chakra is performing, while the former reflects the expression of the third and fourth chakras. Furthermore, consider any physical symptoms, the physical health of organs, as well any psychological symptoms relevant to each chakra when you plan a healing strategy.

Your aura reflects your unique history and consequently how your physical body was impacted by your emotional responses, and therefore the interrelationships between chakras. These therefore affect your overall self-growth and well-being. In other words, as the author Caroline Myss wrote, 'your biography becomes your biology'. Moreover, the level of your personal in this lifetime also impacts your consciousness (past and future incarnations) as well as the entire pool of consciousness you are connected to. As you heal and develop, others around you heal and progress too.

Energy Currents of the HEF

Each energy channel has a purpose or interpretation. Life force energy runs within the Human Energy Field (HEF) in two vertical directions, from one chakra to the next. One is the descending current from the chakra 7 down to the first and is known as the Manifestation Current. The other runs from chakra 1 to the top and is referred to as the Liberation Current (see Figure 16).

As the personality liberates (or releases) and heals the heavy, frozen stuck patterns from the past, energy flows upwards through the chakras, where its frequency increases and awareness expands. We are able to reflect, see the bigger pictures, detect themes and patterns. Consequently, incoming inspiration is received easily. We are able to imagine and visualize what they wish to create in their lives (chakras 7 to 4). As these ideas and thoughts descend to the denser personal chakras, the personality is able to articulate ideas and visions into practical plans and details, and finally take actions to make them real.

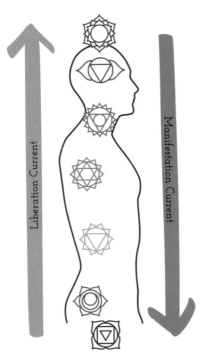

Figure 16: Vertical Energy Currents of the HEF

As seen in Figure 17, there are also two horizontal currents. The first is the incoming current towards each chakra on the front of the body. Depending on how each chakra processes incoming life force, it represents how the individual currently perceives the world. The second type of energy current enters the back chakras and is processed, then subsequently projected outwards, revealing the individual's will to articulate that chakra in the real world. To put it another way, a person's capacity to articulate the essence of a particular chakra practically will be hampered if their perspective is limited.

For instance, someone may be able to receive love and have an open front heart chakra, but they are unable to accept or forgive others (suggesting diminished or closed back chakra). A person can also dream, imagine and receive ideas when the front of the sixth chakra is open but the back is depleted, for instance, but they are unable to materialize such thoughts in the outside world.

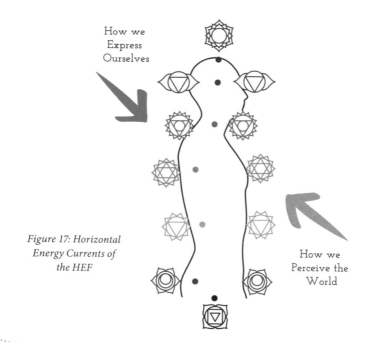

How we
Express
Ourselves

How we
Perceive the
World

Figure 17: Horizontal Energy Currents of the HEF

Assessing Chakras

Healers, when a chakra is slow, or functioning below optimum frequency, can sense or perceive its quality as a murky colour, a cold or coarse sensation, or a slow vibration when they pass their palm over that area. Alternatively, a simple tool to assess chakra functionality is dowsing with a pendulum. An open chakra is assigned a clockwise movement, a troubled chakra will spin in anti-clockwise, and a blocked one will have no movement or rotation. Record your dowsings of the seven chakras below.

CHAKRAS	PENDULUM ROTATION READING ↻ ↺ ↔	
	A (FRONT – PERCEPTION)	B (BACK – WILL)
7		
6		
5		
4		
3		
2		
1		

Figure 18: Pendulum Measurement

Healing Techniques

1 **Forgiveness and Love:** It is more important to accept the facets of ourselves that we have unintentionally rejected throughout our lives when it comes to healing than it is to remove the obstacles. Love and forgiveness are necessary elements for healing. All boundaries are broken down by love, and forgiveness brings about peace and healing. You can pardon individuals who did wrong since they had their own barriers and habits that they failed to overcome, as well as yourself for not making a better decision. As you forgive, peace takes the place of your anger and obstacles, erasing all your patterns permanently. Take a big breath in and let it out completely if you feel a negative emotion starting to arise. Wait a few seconds to regain your balance, then repeat as necessary to achieve quietness and tranquillity. This healing is on a soul level, allowing your consciousness in to help you clear patterns.

2 **Sound Healing:** Mantras are sound power. Mantras are unique vibrational sounds that encourage cell

growth and contraction. They may incorporate sounds of Mandarin Chinese numerals, for example, or age-old healing mantras from other traditions, such as the Sufi Zikr mentioned earlier. Use sounds that correspond to the chakras too. When you are conscious of the pain, you can exhale to the sound of the chakra that corresponds to the area of the pain.

3 **Mind Over Matter:** Mind power is often referred to as mind over matter. Through creative visualization, you can make use of your mind's intelligence to heal your body and your emotions. Imagine or visualize a bright, golden light flowing from the top of your head through your chest and stomach to your lower abdomen. Imagine your cells energized and functioning well. Until you feel better, do this for a few minutes every day and then at least once a week.

4 **Light and Sound:** Combining both is a higher vibration of healing. You can also intuit a colour that you need at any moment and visualize it streaming into your body, as described in the colour visualization, while you chant a mantra or a chakra sound.

5   **Energy Healing:** After dowsing the chakras, you will get a sense of how the energy is moving through them and where it's getting blocked. Decide what you want, relax and regulate your breathing. When you are grounded, you can imagine or pretend that energy is streaming out of your hands to your body. Put your hands on the body part that needs healing or close your eyes and concentrate there mentally. Send healing by visualizing the corresponding colour of the chakra centre you are focusing on.

One technique used effectively is powerful. Combining all the aforementioned methods, exercises and tips, together is more powerful. As long as the issue continues, use these techniques simultaneously for three to five minutes, three to five times per day. The energy barrier will be released as energy flows from the head via the chest and stomach to the lower abdomen, which houses the body's energy reserve. There are more healing tips in the following chapter.

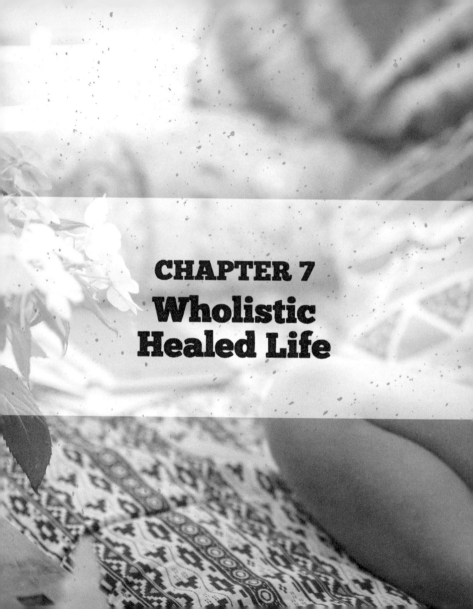

CHAPTER 7
Wholistic Healed Life

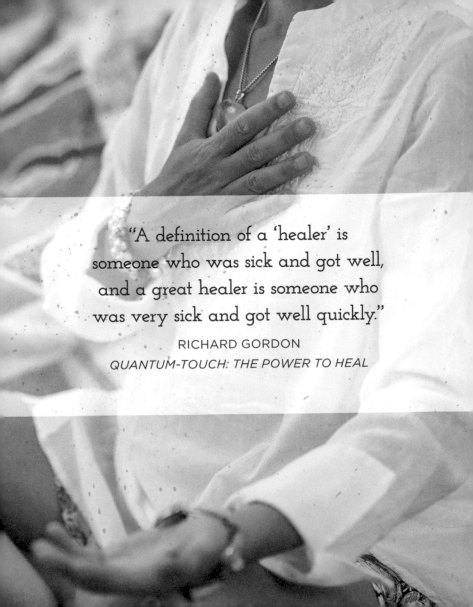

"A definition of a 'healer' is someone who was sick and got well, and a great healer is someone who was very sick and got well quickly."

RICHARD GORDON
QUANTUM-TOUCH: THE POWER TO HEAL

Whatever happened in the past, you can start healing now, in the present moment, by becoming aware of your personal patterns. This awareness necessitates neither judgement nor analysis, but rather loving every aspect of yourself that is in distress. Only then are you able to release it and heal. With daily reflection, healing will happen naturally.

When you judge, you limit yourself and by extension you limit what can be healed within you. However, healing begins when you understand, embrace and love the nature of who you are, and love every atom of your being. Each of us can overcome these constraints only by recognizing our unique identity of consciousness in a physical body, which transcends the narrowness of the self-imposed identity. By opening our minds, we invite the power of universal connection to help heal and live a good life.

Healing distorted patterns is liberation because it allows us to break free from any self-imposed isolation. We engage with the infinite matrix of interconnections and joyful life experiences. It is like plugging into a power grid. The more connected you are, the more power flows to you consistently to heal and achieve your goals. Self-judgement limits our possibilities. However, love and acceptance empower. 'When we love, we always strive to become better than we are,' writes

Paulo Coelho in *The Alchemist* (1988). 'When we strive to become better than we are, everything around us becomes better too.'

Furthermore, recognizing that you are consciousness operating within a physical body, and that both have their own operating dynamic through which they interact, is the first step toward healing your chakras. Understanding how the physical body, mind and the seven chakra system operates is the second step. This understanding allows you to navigate your way through the bumps safely.

Knowing that your consciousness is infinite, and impacts and interacts with other consciousness fields in our universe, is empowering. Sometimes, a dark cloud overhead can shift simply by abandoning your isolation and sitting, for example, under a tree, cuddling your favourite pet at home, or at a busy café sipping a drink. The positive energy field of a passer-by can impact your own, uplifting you instantly, without even speaking a word. Other times, simply by deciding to choose to react or feel differently, you align your energies and healing begins.

Like water, energy flows from high to low. People frequently make the mistake of saying, 'I picked up negative energy from so-and-so…' That is not accurate. Remember that you will react to people at your level. You will resonate with stuck energy if you carry it. Maintaining chakra healing thus necessitates self-awareness. The latter is accomplished by observing what throws you off balance and what gets under your skin, and understanding how actions that you do or do not take spontaneously will either improve or worsen situations in your life.

Holistic Healing and Remedies

Chakra healing entails becoming aware of three factors:

※ How the physical body functions – the seven chakras are linked to the physical body via the hormonal and nervous systems, and how you interpret what happens in your life (the relationship between emotions, mind, and actions).

※ How your energetic being functions – the meaning of the seven personal chakras, the seven energy fields, the four energy currents.

※ How energy and body (your personality) interact: how they influence each other as well as other fields around them.

This one-of-a-kind combination is what distinguishes you as a unique person. And when you are born and given a name, this unique combination begins to develop its own personality, complete with its own energetic imprint or signature, fingerprints, and voice. What you experience as your personality seeps into your consciousness influences its growth.

Furthermore, when your personality is in harmony, consciousness evolves naturally, like an upward spiral towards higher levels of consciousness. So, be mindful of your current feelings, thoughts, and actions. Self-awareness allows your authentic self to naturally emerge and unfold.

When you are developing, you influence and are influenced by your environment. As you heal, your immediate surroundings must be cleared, cleansed or decluttered too. In this way, you and your immediate surroundings are in sync. This includes people, friends and your attitude towards other beings such as animals. Your energy pervades every aspect of your life. You cannot attract new harmonious experiences, just as you cannot store more things in your home or garage, unless you clear out the old. Address what is holding you back at your own pace. The important thing is to make a start, however small that first step is.

YOUR BODY

Simply by paying attention to your physical body, you channel more of your consciousness and mind into your body. The more connected you are with your physical body, the more of your consciousness is present within it. You will manifest your desired goals, and your life will unfold harmoniously, in real time. Healing, and any change you wish for, begins in the present tense. This is why personal awareness is essential. How else can you direct your energy to consciously create what you desire and effect changes in your life, if you are not aware of what is happening in the present moment?

Body awareness allows your authentic self to naturally emerge and unfold, and for your responses to be situationally appropriate. The mind, moreover, is an ethereal quality. Thoughts are energy, and energy is infinite: it extends to the source of all energy. Effectively, your body serves as a vehicle for you to express and manifest your thoughts, goals and desires. Therefore, maintaining your body's wellness is essential for your overall well-being and enjoying your life journey. When body and mind are incompatible, struggle and illness ensue.

Any tension you experience is a natural result of the interaction dynamic between the two forces, energy and matter (in other words, consciousness and body). Constant rebalancing and adjustment are required to maintain harmony in your life. Think of it as an opportunity to heal and rebalance as you move forward. Essentially, dealing with obstacles as they arise in real time empowers you and maintains balanced chakras.

Here are a few tips for looking after your body:

✳ Listen to your body. Focus on your body first thing in the morning and last thing at night.

✳ Give thanks for everything we so easily take for granted. For example, be grateful to your bed for providing comfort, as well as to your feet for allowing you to get out of bed and to your body for working hard and continuously preserving your existence!

✳ Connect with your body several times throughout the day to maintain this awareness. For example, what food does it need? Remember that your body and mind work together to help you achieve your goals throughout the day.

✳ Respect your body by paying attention to its needs and acting on them. This helps in aligning your chakras and

directing your awareness to where change is needed.
Do you, for example, need to rest, relax, eat (healthily),
exercise or meditate?

✳ Focus on the present moment. Be mindful of your current
feelings, thoughts and actions. Keep a journal over a
period of time and track where you are losing your
energy.

STRESS

Listening to your body enables you to embody your consciousness while also providing structure and harmony in your life.
You will experience tangible results with practice, and although
there will be ups and downs because that is the nature of how
the two energies interact, you will recover quickly! However,
regular stress will inadvertently cause many health issue.

Cortisol, the principal stress hormone, raises blood sugar
levels (glucose), improves glucose utilization in the brain,
and increases the availability of chemicals that repair cells.
Cortisol also suppresses functions that would be unnecessary
or detrimental in a fight-or-flight situation. It changes immune
system responses and suppresses the digestive system, repro-
ductive system and development processes. This intricate

natural alarm system also connects with brain regions that affect mood, motivation and fear.

The body's stress response system is normally self-limiting. Hormone levels return to normal once a perceived threat has passed. As your adrenaline and cortisol levels fall, your heart rate and blood pressure return to normal, and other systems resume their normal functions. However, when stressors are continual and you constantly feel under assault, your fight-or-flight response remains activated.

The long-term activation of the stress response system, as well as the subsequent overexposure to cortisol and other stress hormones, can affect nearly all of your body's systems. This increases the risk of a variety of health issues, including:

✳ anxiety/depression

✳ digestive issues

✳ headaches

✳ muscle tightness and discomfort

✳ heart illness, heart attack, high blood pressure, and stroke

✳ sleeping difficulties

✳ weight gain

✳ impaired memory and concentration

That is why it is critical to learn good coping mechanisms for life's stresses. Meditation, creative hobbies and deep breathing intervals throughout your day can help regulate your stress levels.

EMOTIONS

Some of the more painful (emotional) memories can manifest in our bodies as aches and pains. If ignored, they can progress into diseases such as diabetes (lack of sweetness or joy in life), hypertension (as the name implies: prolonged unaddressed tension in our lives), and so on. The way we learn about life and grow is through our emotional responses. Relationships are experimental grounds for our emotions and feelings, demonstrating our range of emotional repones. We swing between extremes, to ascertain our happy point. Intimate relationships are the catalyst for personal or spiritual growth. They can make us feel on top of the world or feel that we hit rock bottom. We learn where our balance point is, what we value and where our happiness and joy lie. They reflect our overall level of consciousness (or awareness) and reflect what we manifest daily.

Caroline Myss writes in her talk *Taking Charge*, 'emotional energy contributes to the formation of cell tissue and forms an energy language that carries literal and symbolic information.' Your biography — that is your life experiences — becomes your biology. She explains 'your body contains your entire life's history — every chapter, line, and verse of every event and relationship. Your biological health becomes a living, breathing biographical statement that conveys your strengths, weaknesses, hopes, and fears as your life progresses.'

When you have an emotional reaction to a problem, you are attempting to integrate your experience and to determine the source of your discomfort or unhappiness. Your reaction is an unconscious reaction to your desire to understand. With understanding comes wisdom. As a result, how you react to change can broaden your understanding and make you a wiser, more enlightened individual. Your emotional evolution is determined by how you process your emotions.

An unresolved negative emotion, moreover, can make you sick and prone to developing cancer. In this instance, forgiveness of the perpetrator and yourself is essential. This is due to the idea that negativity promotes the growth of cancer within the body. Holding onto these unfavourable feelings leads to a persistent state of anxiety, according to Dr Steven Standiford, chief of surgery at the Cancer Treatment Centres of America. An excess of adrenaline and cortisol is produced as a result, and this reduces the production of natural killer cells. Killer cells are what protects us against cancer.

Refusing to forgive not only makes you sick, but it also has the potential to keep you that way. When you think of a painful old memory, such as having been treated unfairly, injured or insulted, your body immediately begins to feel ill as if it is rehappening again in the present moment. Healing can happen only in the present moment, so ask yourself regularly: *Am I living in the present moment, or in the past?*

Therefore, to be in command of your emotional responses is essential. Reflect and ask yourself: *What is this situation showing me?* instead of *why did this happen to me?*. Listen carefully to the advice you receive and have the courage to stay true to yourself by admitting your unhappiness and accepting that you can change your situation to bring you happiness and joy.

THOUGHTS, MIND AND BELIEF SYSTEM

Being in control of our minds is the most difficult aspect of being human. Emotional responses create a belief system, and belief systems attract situations to confirm their validity, making it simple to become stuck and suffer if we are not aware of our patterns. On the other hand, we have free will: the power to decide is our privilege as humans and it is what causes change.

The scientist and mystic Itzahak Bentov believed that our brains do not produce thoughts but are devices for amplifying them. So, when you have an inner conflict, you will attract conflict. How many times have you caught yourself saying: 'I believe my partner does not love me enough' or 'no one appreciates me at work'? What negative thoughts are you amplifying? Become aware of your choice of words, and filter what goes into your brain. Ask yourself: *What belief do I hold, or am I investing in, that supports this drama in my life?* and you will get your answer.

We unconsciously arrange to be right about our beliefs in three ways:

✳ We attract and are attracted to people and situations which confirm our beliefs.

✳ We find ways to distort what we perceive and pick up

interpretations that confirm our beliefs are true.

✳ We act in such manners that compel people to eventually act in such a way that agrees with our beliefs.

If your disappointments are frequent and painful, it is time to pause and ask yourself: *what is within me that is generating a conflict?* Do you have two sets of beliefs that are equally strong, but which contradict each other? For example, do you believe that you really seek true love, but at the same time you know that you will never find it?

Understand that the fundamental purpose of our brain is to predict the future — that is, to learn from past experiences to develop means of getting out of harm's way. If your life seems disappointing, recognize that you do have a choice now, and use it. Allow your past to teach you how to positively influence the present.

Screen false statements and replace them with positive affirmations to build new a belief system. Make a list of old and negative beliefs, and then choose to change them to positive statements in the present tense. These affirmations will help you reframe your beliefs.

Filtering Beliefs

1 Investigate the beliefs that are bothering you. Examine what you are experiencing in these critical areas of your life and determine what beliefs are causing those experiences.

2 Decide whether you want to keep those results.

3 Consider how your views may have influenced the individuals and situations you attract or which attract you.

4 Examine how you occasionally misrepresent what you see or experience to convince yourself that your belief is correct.

5 Reflect on situations in which you behaved to prove to yourself that your belief is accurate.

6 Explore emotional past experiences that may have led you to form negative beliefs.

7 Mindfully design belief statements that work for your benefit in all the areas in your life (see Figure 19), using the present tense.

8 Rewrite the new belief as a succinct positive statement, in the present tense, affirming your new belief.

9 Repeat your affirmations out loud 28 times each day, for at least 21 days.

10 Afterwards, close your eyes and visualize the result of believing your new belief and the emotional relief it brings, and feel that you are enjoying these results.

11 It is advisable that you work on a maximum of three affirmations at any time. Once your brain registers them, your experiences will start changing, which then lets you move to other affirmations.

ACTIONS

When you are self-aware and connected to your essence as a consciousness in a body, you will naturally align with your life path, and your journey will become smoother and more

Life Area	Current Belief	New Positive Belief	Positive Affirmation for that Belief
Self-esteem			
Self-worth			
Personal Abilities			
Competence			
Career			
Ability to Manifest			
Relationships			
Authority Figures			
Money and Prosperity			
Physical and Mental Health			
Your Spiritual Belief			

Figure 19: Creating New Beliefs and Affirmations

peaceful. Indeed, almost magical! As you mindfully guide it, life will unfold before you like a carpet unrolling. All of the missing pieces, including your desires and wellness goals, will fall into place naturally.

Your actions stem from your conscious and unconscious beliefs. Before taking any action, your brain processes the information it already has, to predict an outcome. This is referred to as the thinking process. Your way of thinking is influenced by how much you pay attention to your life, and how much you have learned from your past — and thinking takes places in the present. Moreover, how you feel also affects how you think because it is connected to your belief system. A negative mindset, for example, limits your self-awareness and therefore any actions you take.

Furthermore, your brain uses knowledge you already have. The more open-minded you are and curious, the more flexible your action will be. If your brain is missing a piece of a puzzle, your actions will be limited because they will be based on what you already know rather on other means you can explore. Therefore, a relaxed and curious mind is vital!

Science confirms that meditation, for example, is an effective tool to relax the mind and expand awareness. So, take time to cool down before you respond, and make any decisions that can impact your energy field and life adversely. Energetically speaking, the goal of meditation is to achieve a balanced flow of energy in our system. Moving mediation, such as Tai Chi or Chi Qing, may help active or hyperactive individuals attain equilibrium, while quieter individuals may benefit from quieter mediation techniques such as Zen or transcendental meditation.

Creative meditation is a guided visualization technique which involves a variety of tools such as breathing, visualization, psychic and energy exercises, making it fun and safe to practise for both types of individual. Experiment with listening to guided mediations, or meditations that combine binaural sounds.

Daily meditation enhances brain function, reduces stress and allows you to connect intimately with your inner self, the people around you, and your inner senses. With practice, you will be able to maintain a level of peace and tranquillity. No matter what comes your way, you will deal with it calmly.

Any simple activity, pastime, or pursuit that you enjoy might induce a meditative state and allows your brain to develop a coherent thinking process. It does not have to have a grand title in order for you to receive the benefits. If one doesn't appear to work for you, try a different one that does.

Ultimately, taking the decision to make new changes in your life is entirely up to you. Simple affirmations such as the following can help you begin the process: 'I choose to react differently. I chose to feel differently.' Disrupt existing negative patterns by actually taking a different action instead your usual response. With practice, this will begin to come naturally to you.

Quick Fixes

1. Creativity

Any quietness, or me-time, such as focusing on your breath or a creative hobby you practise on your own, allows you to feel tranquil while simultaneously raising your vibration. As you are having fun, your aura expands, and all the stuck energy falls away. In fact, when you learn anything new it 'modifies the physical structure of the brain,' according to the National Academic Press of Sciences, Engineering, and Medicine. Structure alterations have an impact on the functional organisation of the brain.

Learning organizes and reorganizes the brain. 'At different periods, different areas of the brain may be ready to learn.' If you choose to express yourself creatively by playing a beautiful piece of music on a guitar, or listening to music, your brain's attention moves from acute concentration on an issue preoccupying you to sections of the brain that are more involved in emotional content and auditory processing. And when you are not paying attention to your problem, an epiphany may occur and resolve your conundrum. So, rather than remaining stuck, start a new hobby.

2. Perfume, Music, Visually Pleasing Images and Pets

Figure 20 indicates the different areas of the brain that perceive information from our five senses. The optic nerves and the olfactory system connect to the centre of the brain. The auditory nervous system connects the cochlea to a station in the brainstem (known as the nucleus).

Neural impulses pass from that station to the brain, notably the temporal lobe, where sound is attached, meaning that we hear. Moreover, sensations start as messages from touch receptors in your skin. They move along sensory nerves, which are made up of bundled fibres that connect to neurons in the spinal cord. The information is then relayed to the remainder of the brain by the thalamus.

Using scents, listening to music, looking at pictures of pleasurable scenery (or chakra colours), for example, and even stroking your pet send immediate messages to your brain, causing you to relax and change your mood or raise your

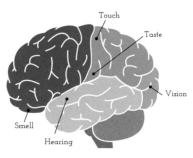

Figure 20: Brain Areas of Perceiving Through the Five Senses

vibration. These are examples of simple action you can chose to rebalance your energy quickly.

The power of your own voice when you chant the chakra healing sounds in Figure 7 (page 57) for example, reverberates throughout your whole body, clearing and realigning your energy centres right away. With regular practice, you will be to maintain a clear and balanced aura.

3. Sound Essences

When your upper chakras are well developed, you will be able perceive the energy of organs or chakras through vibration, or sound. On that level, sound healing can be very effective as the etheric layer holds the blue-print template of all the physical body.

Illness, or dies-ease, are frequency imbalances which are typically caused by a blockage in one or more channels on any of the auric centres or layers. Our energy field, meridians, arteries, veins, lymph and/or nerves and even our emotional and mental state are all part of this. Dr R Gerber, author of *Vibrational Medicine: The #1 Handbook of Subtle-energy Therapies*, coined the term 'vibrational medicine' to designate any form of alternative healthcare that attempts to treat variables in a client that cause conflict in the flow of vital energy.

In addition, the objective of vibrational medicine is to move, unblock or balance life energy throughout the physical, energetic and spiritual bodies. Sound Essences are unique vibrational remedies that have been charged with sound waves to assist in rebalancing body energy. They are simple to apply, have lovely smells and are effective. Spray your energy field with the suitable remedy, or set of remedies, once a day.

Sound Essences sprays are infused with the healing vibrations found in Sound, Colour, Crystals and Gems, Positive Word Affirmations, Sacred Geometry, Symbols, Aroma, and Homeopathy, and were developed by Evelyn Mulders, the founder of the Kinesiology College of Canada and senior faculty for the International College of Professional Kinesiology Practice, who has been training students in Energy Medicine since 1996.

Their healing vibrations connect with the physical and energetic bodies, resulting in full spectrum vibrational healing for energy balance. Evelyn believes that the secret of balancing chakras is vibrationally supporting the seven senses related to the seven chakras (see Figure 21). Sound Essences are worth investigating in order to assist you in maintaining the energy structure of your aura as you heal and balance till you accomplish your objective (see www.soundessence.net).

CHAKRA	SENSE	HOLISTIC THERAPY
Root	Smell	Aromatherapy
Sacral	Taste	Foods, Herbs, Homeopathy, Flower, Sea, Gem and Sound Essences
Solar Plexus	Sight	Symbology and Sacred Geometry
Heart	Feel	Healing Touch, Crystals and Gems
Throat	Sound	Music and Yantras
Brow	Light & Colour	Colour Therapy
Crown	Thought	Prayer, Mantras and Positive Affirmation

Figure 21: Chakras, Senses and Related Therapies, Courtesy of Evelyn Mulders

It is important to make steady, small-step improvements when healing. By doing this, you will avoid fighting with yourself unintentionally, which is what happens when our brains adapt to new situations. By sticking to what you already know, the brain tries to keep you safe by interpreting unexpected changes as threats. Keep in mind that chakra healing is a journey rather than a destination. Be kind to yourself because it takes time to correct or change ingrained patterns of discord or energetic obstacles.

When daily awareness becomes a lifestyle, or self-love habit, you will find that you recover more easily, and life flows magically. In other words, you develop personal resilience. 'It's not that I don't get thrown off,' said Morihei Ueshiba (1883–1969), the founder of Aikido, 'but I recover so quickly you don't notice I was away.'

4. Daily Chakra Visualization

This daily visualization aids in chakra cleansing and aura balance restoration.

Imagine that you are tanning under a sun that changes its colour as and when it is required. Take a few deep breaths and settle into a relaxing breathing pattern. Imagine lying down under a red sun and breathing in red light till each cell is re-energized. Note your feelings as you go through this visualization.

When you are ready, the sun changes to an orange colour. Now its orange fall on your body, completely penetrating each cell. Enjoy this pleasant, loving sensation. As you continue to sunbathe under your imaginary sun, imagine or pretend that the sun's colour changes once more to yellow, then to green, blue, and so on. Move to the next colour when you feel that your body has absorbed all it needs.

Observe any changes that occur as you sunbathe with each colour. Make a mental note of how you feel with under each colour — if you feel heavy or light, relaxed or energized and which body part or organs absorbed each colour most.

Conclusion

In conclusion, the purpose of this book is not to diagnose but to empower you to know yourself on a deeper level by understanding the energy flow through the chakras, their physiological impact, as well as the need for a wholistic solution to heal effectively. And by recognizing that you are a unique combination of consciousness and physical body, which is not limited by the personality. The key to directing your consciousness is your mind. Transformation occurs when you hold yourself accountable, take charge of your own healing and design your own well-being fulfilling your life's purpose joyfully.

The journey of the healer is the start of:

✳ self-empowerment;

✳ self-knowledge; *and*

✳ self-responsibility.

Moreover, self-awareness is not a hobby, so be patient with

yourself. Reflecting and understanding are daily commitments that will help you advance your wisdom.

We hope that the ideas presented here have motivated you to observe yourself lovingly and gain clarity, knowing that the greatest healing force is (unconditional) love.

May the Healing Light always shine on you.

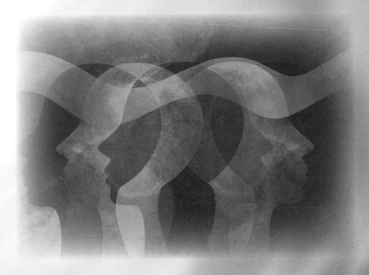

Table of Figures

Further Reading

Brennan, Barbara Ann. *Hands of Light, A Guide to Healing Through the Human Energy Field*, Random House Publishing Group (1987).

Gerber, R., *Vibrational Medicine: The #1 Handbook of Subtle-energy Therapies* (Bear & Company, 2001)

Hay, Louise L. *Heal Your Body: The Mental Causes of Physical Illness and the Metaphysical Way to Overcome Them*, (Hay House 1984)

Huneidi-Palmer, Sahar. *Your Psychic Power*, Arcturus Publishing (2022).

Mulders, Evelyn. *The Essence of Sound: Full Spectrum Vibrational Healing for Meridians, Chakras, Auric Field, & Figure Eight Energies*, Satiama Publishing (2020).

Wolfe, Amber. *Personal Alchemy: A Handbook of Healing and Self-Transformation*; Llewellyn Publications (1993).